剑桥双语分级阅读·小说馆（第2版）

原版系列编辑 Nicholas Tims

U1009365

Bullring Kid and Country Cowboy

斗牛场酷妞与乡村牛仔

[英] 路易丝·克洛弗 著

王文赞 编译

李丽华 审订

北京语言大学出版社
BEIJING LANGUAGE AND CULTURE UNIVERSITY PRESS

CAMBRIDGE UNIVERSITY PRESS

社图号25009

北京市版权局著作权合同登记图字：01-2024-3256号

图书在版编目（CIP）数据

斗牛场酷妞与乡村牛仔 ： 英汉对照 / （英）路易丝·克洛弗（Louise Clover）著 ； 王文赞编译. -- 2版. 北京 ： 北京语言大学出版社，2025. 3. -- (剑桥双语分级阅读小说馆). -- ISBN 978-7-5619-6728-7

Ⅰ. H319.4

中国国家版本馆CIP数据核字第2025QP0233号

斗牛场酷妞与乡村牛仔
DOUNIUCHANG KU NIU YU XIANGCUN NIUZAI

责任编辑：赵敏亚
责任印制：周 燚

出版发行：北京语言大学出版社
社　　址：北京市海淀区学院路 15 号，100083
网　　址：www.blcup.com
电子信箱：service@blcup.com
电　　话：编 辑 部 010-8230 1019
　　　　　发 行 部 010-8230 3650/3591/3648
　　　　　北语书店 010-8230 3653
　　　　　网购咨询 010-8230 3908
印　　刷：东港股份有限公司

版　　次：2017 年 6 月第 1 版　2025 年 3 月第 2 版　印　　次：2025 年 3 月第 1 次印刷
开　　本：880 毫米 × 1230 毫米　1/32　印　　张：6.875
字　　数：162 千字　定　　价：23.00 元

PRINTED IN CHINA
凡有印装质量问题，本社负责调换。售后QQ号1367565611，电话010-82303590

Preface

前言

“剑桥双语分级阅读 · 小说馆”是一套从剑桥大学出版社引进的面向非英语国家英语学习者的分级系列读物，由英语语言教学专家及小说作家合力创作。创作过程历时三十余年，出版后受到世界各地英语教师和英语学习者的喜爱，许多读本再版多次，三十余年来畅销不衰，成为受全球英语学习者青睐的优秀读本。

本系列读物具有以下突出特色：

1. 是原创英语读物，而非改编自普通作品的读物。因此，阅读本系列读物，我们读到的是原汁原味的原创英语，而非人为改编过的二手英语。

2. 是当代优秀短篇小说，而非年代久远的小说。因此，阅读本系列读物，我们读到的是当今鲜活的、学了就能用的英语，而非穿越时空的、学了用不上的英语；了解的是与读者同时代不同国家人们的生活和思想，而非隔代人的生活、文化和风土人情。

3. 是专为非英语国家的英语学习者量身定制的读物，而非为英语母语者所写的大众读物。因此，本系列读物是中国读者首选的英语学习读物。

4. 是英美知名小说家和英语语言教学专家合力创作的读物。小说家保障了读物的可读性与可欣赏性，英语语言教学专家保障了读物语言作为英语习得材料的科学性与可学性。本系列读物中的多个读本都曾在世界上颇具影响力的“语言学习者文学奖”（Language Learner Literature Award）评选中获得大奖。因此，阅读本系列读物，我们会在欣赏小说的同时，自然而然地、有效地提高自己的英语水平。

5. 本系列读物的故事题材丰富多样，包括侦探、情感、历险、悬疑、人文、科幻、喜剧等，读者可以随心选择自己喜欢的类别阅读；故事内容生动有趣，故事情节引人入胜、扣人心弦，读者一旦开始阅读，就想一口气读完，使阅读真正升华到“悦读”。

6. 随书附赠的音频材料内容精彩，是专业配音员的演绎再创作。听着它，我们犹如在听广播剧、听评书，又仿佛是在听电影、听话剧……这种聆听英语的享受将彻底扫除学生对英语听力的畏难心理。

7. 本系列读物所使用的语言，既有英式英语，也有美式英语，对应的音频材料也相应分为英音和美音，读者可根据自己的喜好来选择。

8. 本系列近百本读物根据《欧洲语言共同参考框架》(CEFR)和剑桥大学外语考评部开发的 ESOL 考试的标准来确定级别划分，是建立在科学研究和实践基础之上的分级。全套共分七个级别（与中国学生英语基础水平的大致对应关系，请参见图书封底表格），读者可根据自己的英语基础选择相应级别的读本来学习。

为了更好地帮助中国学生学习和欣赏，“剑桥双语分级阅读·小说馆”从剑桥大学出版社原版引进后又增加了以下内容：

1. 增加了适量的辅助学习内容，包括“读前思考”“读后活动”“学习指导”三个板块，其中“学习指导”板块又包括生词、短语和表达、文化点滴、阅读练习四项内容。增加这些板块的目的是全方位帮助学生提升英语阅读能力，扩充词汇量，扫除阅读中的文化障碍，增强对英语小说的鉴赏能力。

2. 增加了小说全文的参考译文。出于语言学习的考虑，译文多采用直译，但也尽量符合中文的表达习惯。

值得一提的是，所增加的辅助学习内容和参考译文，全部由来自全国不同省市知名中学（包括人大附中、北大附中、清华附中、黄冈中学、上海中学等三十余所中学）的一线英语教师完成。这些一线教师的加盟，确保了所加内容与中国学生的英语学习特点和学习需求相吻合，为学生阅读和欣赏读物、提高英语水平给予恰到好处的助力。

英语阅读是英语课堂的延伸和补充，也是培养英语语感、提高英语水平的有效途径。选择一套好的英语读物，收获的将不仅仅是语言的进步。欢迎年轻朋友们来到“剑桥双语分级阅读·小说馆”，打开一本本好书，品味一个个好故事，为实现梦想搭建桥梁。

北京语言大学出版社

Contents 目录

People in the story

故事中的人物

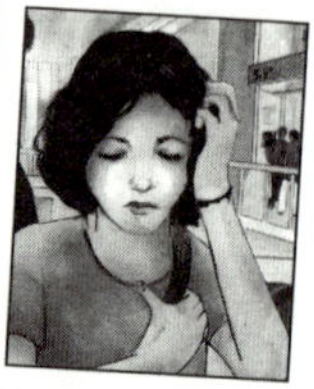

Fizza McIntyre: a fifteen-year-old girl from Birmingham

菲扎·麦金太尔：来自伯明翰的 15 岁女孩儿

Fletcher McIntyre: a fifteen-year-old boy from the small island of Sark

弗莱彻·麦金太尔：来自萨克小岛的 15 岁男孩儿

Imran McIntyre: Fizza's dad

依姆兰·麦金太尔：菲扎的爸爸

Rubel McIntyre: Fizza's mum

鲁贝尔·麦金太尔：菲扎的妈妈

Richard McIntyre: Fletcher's dad

理查德·麦金太尔：弗莱彻的爸爸

Babs: Fizza's best friend

芭布丝：菲扎最好的朋友

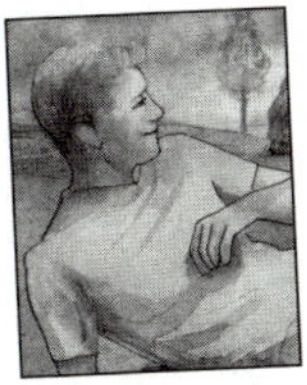

Billy Adams: one of the most popular boys at Fizza's school

比利·亚当斯：菲扎学校里最受欢迎的男孩儿之一

Robert Scully: a rich businessman

罗伯特·斯库利：一位富商

Before reading

读前思考

Look at the cover and the pictures in the first two chapters. Answer the question.

Do you think that Fizza is the Country Cowboy?

____

Chapter 1
The Judo Kid

'Oof!'

For the fifth time, Fizza's dad threw her over his back and onto the grass.

'Ow! I wasn't ready, Dad!' she cried.

'That's no excuse, Fizza! You must always be ready!' replied her father. 'You might be a girl – but it doesn't stop you from being as brave as a man.'

Fizza picked herself up from the ground and faced her judo teacher. Imran McIntyre was half-Scottish, half-Pakistani, and one hundred percent crazy. They had been practising judo for over an hour in the late afternoon sunshine and she was getting really tired now. However, she still managed to take her dad by surprise. Although she was feeling weak, she suddenly ran at him and threw him to the ground.

'Fizza! Leave your poor father alone!' called her mother from the house. 'Anyway, it's time for tea.'

'Thanks, Rubel! You saved me from the crazy judo kid!' said Imran.

He got up and took Fizza's hand and, laughing together, they went into the house.

It was Thursday, so Fizza knew what her mum had made for tea. Every week it was the same, because it was her dad's favourite meal.

'Oh no, I hate fish curry!' thought Fizza as she sat down at the table.

The fish curry was always so hot it set her mouth on fire – and she *hated* fish. However, to keep her mum and dad happy, she ate her food without complaining.

'So are you looking forward to our holiday, Fizza?' asked her dad.

'No—,' thought Fizza.

'Yes, she is!' interrupted her mum. 'Aren't you, darling?'

Fizza smiled falsely through a horrible mouthful of curry.

'I can't wait! I love the Channel Islands, but this will be the first time I've been to Sark,' said Fizza's dad as he greedily took another big spoonful of food from the bowl. 'It's the smallest of the islands, isn't it?'

'Yes, and no cars are allowed there, so it's going to be quiet! Fresh air and no pollution!' said her mum.

'How wonderful!' said Imran.

'How boring!' thought Fizza.

Fizza's mum, Rubel, worked for Birmingham Council in the Environmental Office. It was her job to make Birmingham cleaner and 'greener', but it was a difficult job with so many cars and factories in the city. There was also too much rubbish. So a holiday on an island with no cars was her idea of a perfect holiday. However, it was not Fizza's idea of a perfect holiday. She loved the city. She loved Birmingham! It was busy! It was loud! It was home!

'Right!' said Imran, as he finished his meal. 'Come on, Fizza – let's practise some more judo.'

'But I wanted to go on the computer,' said Fizza.

'Felicity,' said her mum, 'you're always on that computer.'

It was true. Fizza loved her computer. She spent hours working on different programs and she was the best in her class at information technology. It was the one school subject that she knew she was good at.

'But I want to talk to my friends,' she replied.

'Can't you use the phone?' said her mum. 'Or better still, go and visit them – like I did when I was a girl.'

'And you won't get any better at judo unless you

practise!' said her dad.

Fizza sighed deeply. It was always the same thing. Her mum thought she used her computer too much and her dad thought that she should be an Olympic judo champion.

Fizza's dad thought that judo was the most important thing in the world. When he wasn't practising it, he was talking about it. He had taken up judo as a small boy and eventually he had become National Champion of Scotland. However, Fizza did not love it as much as her dad.

'Actually Fizza, I think you're really making progress now,' he said. 'You'll be a champion yet! But I've told you before, you should join a judo club!'

Once again Fizza sighed. She didn't mind practising in the garden, but she didn't want to join a judo club because judo wasn't 'cool'. Her best friend Babs didn't do judo and nor did any of the other 'cool' girls.

'Dad! Are you crazy?' she said.

'I'm sorry?' said her father.

'You teach me everything. What else can a club teach me?' said Fizza.

Imran laughed at this sweet talk and Fizza jumped

up from the table.

'Come on, old man. Let's have a race to the garden – and I promise I'll be gentle with you!'

* * *

At about six thirty, the doorbell rang.

'Fizza!' her mum called up the stairs. 'Babs is here!'

Fizza ran down the stairs. Her friend was waiting for her in the hall.

'Hi, Babs!' she said.

'Fizza! I had to come and tell you something!' said Babs, who was clearly very excited.

'Oh? What is it?'

'I've just been to the shops and guess who was on the bus!' she said.

'The Queen?'

'What? No, don't be silly. Billy Adams!'

'Who?'

'Fizza! You know! He's that seriously good-looking guy at school!'

Babs wanted to go out with Billy, but so did all the girls in their year. He was very popular with girls.

'And?' said Fizza.

'And what?' replied Babs.

'Well, what happened?'

'Well, he looked at me. Well, I *think* he looked at me – he looked near me because he sat in front of me.'

'And he had the whole of the bus to choose from?'

'Yeah!'

Fizza didn't like to say it was probably just chance that Billy had sat in front of her.

'Wow!' she replied.

'I know!' said Babs.

Fizza smiled. She had been good friends with Babs since they had joined the school at the age of eleven. For four years they had done everything together: laughed, played silly games, shared secrets, and laughed some more. However, recently Fizza felt that something had changed, because something new had arrived in Babs's life. In fact two things had arrived: boys and fashion. Babs had stopped wearing school uniform and she had started dressing in the same way as the frightening 'cool' girls. And although Fizza secretly wanted to be 'cool', she *did* still wear school uniform and outside of school she just wore jeans, T-shirts, and trainers. She wasn't really interested in wearing silly clothes or makeup – especially for boys.

Fizza's mum said that she was pretty but then, she thought, her mum would say that, wouldn't she? She had thick, black hair which she always wore tied back, brown eyes, a button nose and a mouth which she thought made her look like a frog. It didn't help that she was small and thin for a fifteen-year-old, because it made her look younger than all the other girls.

Fizza knew she and Babs could still be friends and they could still share secrets. But the secrets were different now. They weren't about sweet baby animals or a house with a ghost at the end of the street. They were about boys like Billy.

'Well,' said Fizza. 'He'll be at school tomorrow!'

'Ooh! I know! I know!' said Babs. 'I can't wait! I'm going to make myself talk to him! And Fizza, you're going to help me!'

Chapter 2

Fizza is cool for ten minutes

The next day was the last day of the school term and there were no proper classes. No one was going to do any work that day. Hundreds of children moved from class to class, talking excitedly about their summer holidays. Fizza sat in the computer classroom and listened. She heard about trips to Disneyland, summer camps in America, and holidays in Spain, Italy and Portugal. Babs was telling a group of the frightening 'cool' girls in their class about her sailing holiday with her cousins in Greece. Fizza pretended to be busy working at the computer so she didn't have to tell anyone about her holiday on the very quiet, pollution-free island of Sark.

Suddenly four boys ran into the classroom, laughing and shouting. Fizza noticed that one of them was Billy Adams, the 'seriously good-looking guy' that Babs had seen on the bus the evening before. Fizza smiled to herself when she saw Babs cover her face with her hands in embarrassment. The group of 'cool' girls whispered to one another in excitement at the boys' arrival. These boys didn't care about school; they just wanted to have a laugh. They were always in trouble with the teachers, which made them even more attractive to girls. Fizza hid shyly behind her computer.

'Who's good at computers in here?' asked Billy.

The girls looked at one another. They all knew how to use chatrooms but not much else.

'Why?' asked one of them.

'I need help with some pictures.'

'I know who can help you, Billy!' someone said in a voice that was a bit too high and a bit too loud.

Fizza looked out from behind her computer to see who had spoken; she was surprised to see it was a very red-faced Babs. And when Billy Adams turned to look at her, she turned from red to purple! Fizza thought her poor friend was about to explode with embarrassment.

'Yeah?' he said.

'Fizza.'

'Who?' said Billy.

Babs pointed at Fizza.

'That's Fizza. She's brilliant with computers.'

Everyone looked at Fizza. She wanted to hide under her desk.

'Oh, great. Thanks,' said Billy and walked over to where Fizza was sitting.

'Hi, Fizza,' he said.

'Hi,' she managed to whisper.

'Could you do something with this?' said Billy as he sat down next to her and gave her a CD. She stared at it.

'It's pictures of the teachers,' he said, smiling. 'I want to give them an end-of-term "present".'

Fizza put the CD into the computer. After a moment pictures of all their teachers appeared.

'Now, Fizza,' said Billy, moving closer to her.

He was so close she could feel his breath on her cheek and it smelled of chewing gum. She had to admit to herself that he *was* good-looking: he had clear blue eyes and short fair hair and a gentle smile. However, she kept staring at the computer screen; she was far too shy to look at him directly.

'Do you think you could put *his* head on *her* body?' Billy continued.

He pointed at a picture of Mr Roberts, their science teacher, who wore glasses and had hardly any hair. Then he pointed at Miss Simmons, the English teacher, who was small and fat and wore a bright pink dress. Fizza smiled. She thought it was a really funny idea.

'Of course I can,' she said and she began to work.

Once she had finished with Mr Roberts and Miss Simmons, she moved on to Miss Brown, the very slim and pretty history teacher. Miss Brown received the headmaster's head and the hairy legs of the sports teacher. By the time she had finished with Mr Jones, the poor maths teacher, he was wearing a short skirt and had a long, grey beard.

'Amazing!' said Billy as everyone crowded round the computer screen.

He then turned to Fizza, looked directly at her and smiled.

'Thanks, Fizza, you're really cool,' he said.

Then the boys left the classroom and the frightening girls stared at Fizza. They obviously couldn't believe that dull Fizza McIntyre had been given so much attention by the wonderful Billy Adams.

'Wow! I can't believe it!' whispered Babs, as she sat down next to Fizza.

Fizza smiled back at her; she couldn't believe it either. One of the coolest boys in the school had called her cool!

'Fizza! Listen! Do you think Billy likes me?' said Babs. 'He *did* speak to me!'

'I'm sure he likes you,' said Fizza. 'Who wouldn't?'

And smiling to herself, she turned back to the computer screen.

*　*　*

It was the second week of the school holidays and Fizza was at the shops with her mum. They were in the Bullring Shopping Centre in Birmingham.

She was feeling a bit strange because she had just had her hair cut. Her mum and the hairdresser had both agreed that her new haircut looked fantastic.

'But then,' Fizza thought, 'they would say that, wouldn't they?'

She didn't really care what they thought, because secretly she had had her hair cut for someone else. Fizza McIntyre didn't want to admit it to anyone, but something had changed inside her. Every day since the end of term, she had looked at herself in her bedroom mirror.

'He called me cool,' she told the mirror. 'He called me cool.'

The truth was she wanted to look 'cool' not for herself – but for Billy Adams.

The shopping centre was full of bored teenagers wasting time in their school holidays. As she followed her mum out of a shoe shop, she turned a corner and walked straight into a group of boys from school. In the middle of them was Billy Adams!

Fizza could feel her face getting hot. She wanted to run and hide. She wanted to be somewhere else, anywhere but right there at that moment in the Bullring Shopping Centre. Then she remembered what her dad told her every time they practised judo.

'Fizza, you might be a girl,' he said, 'but it doesn't stop you from being as brave as a man.'

So she made herself be brave. She looked straight at Billy and gave him a great big smile.

'Hello, Billy,' she said.

Billy looked at her ... and then he looked away.

'Who's that?' Fizza heard one of his friends say to him.

'I don't know,' replied Billy.

Fizza felt terrible. Billy didn't want to know her! She could feel hot tears in her eyes and she wanted to run away, but she couldn't – she had to walk, she had to be 'cool.'

'Me? Cool?' she thought. 'Forget it.'

For the first time, she was really glad that she was going away to the island of Sark and she followed her mother out of the shopping centre as quickly as she could.

However, Fizza didn't know that Billy Adams was watching her walk away. He hadn't recognised her with her new haircut – but he had thought that she was a very pretty girl.

Chapter 3
The island that time forgot

Fizza looked out across the field from the white cottage that she was sharing with her mum and dad. She looked along the rocky coast. Then she looked at the boats parked in a tidy line in the little harbour down below. The boat that they had arrived on earlier in the day was just beginning its return journey to the island of Guernsey and she watched it disappear across the deep blue sea, shining in the afternoon sunshine. To her left, coming up the hill, she could see a large brown horse pulling a carriage full of tourists, and in the distance she saw a man driving a tractor across a field. Fizza McIntyre could see lots of things, but she couldn't hear anything. The island of Sark was quiet – deadly quiet. It was so quiet it made Fizza feel uncomfortable. However, her mum was feeling very comfortable!

'Isn't this exciting, Fizza!' said Rubel McIntyre, coming out of the cottage door, drying her hands on a towel. 'You can just smell the peace, can't you?'

Fizza pretended to yawn. 'Exciting' was the last word she would use to describe this place. She already knew that this holiday was going to be the most boring one ever.

She kicked a stone, which unfortunately hit her mum's foot.

'Ow! Look out! Why are you so cross, young lady?'

'Sorry, Mum. I'm just tired. Sorry.'

Fizza was in a bad mood, but she was tired too. They had started their journey from Birmingham at six o'clock that morning. They had driven for four hours to catch the boat to Guernsey. Then they had taken a smaller boat to Sark, where they had been met by a horse and carriage! Eventually they had arrived at a cottage which didn't even have a television – and there was certainly no Internet. Fizza knew that this holiday was going to be a complete failure! She was even looking forward to going back to school!

However, there had been one thing that had made Fizza smile a little bit that day.

As their boat arrived that morning, all the passengers had been met by a queue of horses and carriages – the island's taxi service. Their 'taxi' was from 'The Richard

McIntyre Horse and Carriage Company' and their driver was a tall man in his forties, with curly brown hair and a happy suntanned face.

'Hello! My name is Richard McIntyre,' he had said.

'And I'm Imran McIntyre!' Fizza's dad had laughed. 'What are the chances of that!'

'We've come all this way only to meet someone with exactly the same surname!' her mum had said.

And everyone had laughed, including Fizza, as Richard McIntyre put their suitcases onto the carriage and drove them up the hill.

'Where are you from?' he had asked.

'Birmingham.'

'Ah, Birmingham – a bit different from Sark, I imagine.'

'Yes. It's big! It's noisy!' her mum had answered.

'It's great!' Fizza had thought.

'And what about pollution?' asked Richard. 'On Sark we have no cars, so we have almost no pollution!'

'Oh yes,' her mum had said, 'I'm sorry to say we have a lot of pollution in Birmingham.'

'We also have a lot of nice things to do in Birmingham,' Fizza had thought, staring out of the back of the carriage and wondering what Billy Adams was doing at that moment. He wasn't on some silly, smelly horse carriage – she was certain of that.

'Oh, you'll love Sark! They call it the island that time forgot,' Richard had said.

'I wish I could forget about it,' Fizza had thought.

* * *

And so it was that Fizza found herself on 'the island that time forgot' with absolutely nothing to do. Her mum's voice brought her out of her dream and back to the present moment.

'Why don't you go and explore, Fizza?' said her mum. 'By the time you get back, I'll have supper ready. Oh! And get your dad a newspaper, please.'

Fizza went down the hill towards the little village at the bottom. In five minutes she had discovered two bicycle hire shops, three shops that sold jewellery and jugs, and a tiny post office which was also a supermarket. Fizza went up to the counter.

'Do you sell newspapers?' she asked a small grey-haired lady.

'Sorry,' she said, 'they haven't arrived from Guernsey today. Try tomorrow.'

'What is this place?' thought Fizza. 'There aren't even any newspapers!'

She thanked the lady and left the shop. As she began the climb back up the hill, she passed a group of girls of about her age. They were chewing gum and wearing short skirts. They looked just like the 'cool' girls from school, which made Fizza smile.

'Some things never change,' she thought, 'wherever you go.'

And she began to run back towards the cottage.

Later, after supper, Fizza and her dad practised judo in the field behind the cottage. For over an hour they threw one another onto the grass until Imran admitted defeat and went inside to play a game of cards with Rubel.

As the sun began to drop down from the sky like a great big orange, Fizza continued to practise her judo moves. Eventually she got tired and stopped. She looked out at the dark grey sea and breathed in deeply. And for the first time since she had arrived on Sark, she found herself listening. She could hear the birds singing good night to each other, and the sound of sheep bells and a boat in the distance. Then, lifting her nose into the air, she breathed in deeply and she found that the evening air of Sark smelled sweet. It was completely different from the heavy city smell of her much-loved Birmingham. Such beauty suddenly made Fizza McIntyre feel alive and she decided to show the island how good she felt.

'Good night, Sark!' she shouted as she jumped high in the air and then fell on the grass.

Laughing at herself for being silly, she picked herself up and turned to go indoors, but immediately she came to a stop.

Sitting in a tree beside the cottage was a red-haired boy who looked about the same age as her. For a moment they stared at one another until her attention was taken by a small brown rabbit that ran past her. She took her eyes away from the boy for just a few seconds and during this time he completely disappeared.

Chapter 4
Fizza meets Fletcher

The next morning Fizza was woken up by her mother.

'Come on, you lazy lady! Get up! Richard's outside – he's going to take us on a tour of the island!'

Fizza opened one eye and looked at her watch. It said seven o'clock. 'Mum! I'm on holiday!' she said as she put her pillow over her head.

'Come on! Richard says it's the best time of day to see the island – before it gets too crowded.'

'Crowded? Here?' thought Fizza. 'That doesn't seem likely.'

Eventually, when she had washed, brushed her teeth and quickly eaten some breakfast, she stepped outside. Her mum, dad, and Richard McIntyre and his horse and carriage were waiting for her.

'Good morning, young lady!' he said cheerfully.

'Is it?' asked Fizza, yawning.

'Of course it is!' Richard laughed. 'The sun's out!

So are you ready?'

'Yeah, I'm ready ...' said Fizza.

She wondered if Richard McIntyre was always this happy. Still sleepy, she climbed up on the carriage and they began their journey across the island.

For the next few hours the carriage moved slowly past trees, fields, a few houses and tractors. It also moved past other carriages carrying tourists. They saw small beaches, rocks on the coast and black holes, which Richard said were caves. They went from Derrible Bay to Dixcart Bay, and then past a large golden beach at La Grand Grève. The adults talked about the countryside and about towns, and Rubel McIntyre told Richard about her job as an environmental officer.

'I think that Birmingham could learn something from Sark,' she said.

'Well, why don't you start by getting rid of all the cars and telling everyone to buy a horse?' said Richard.

And they all laughed apart from Fizza, who was beginning to feel sick at the back of the carriage.

They continued their journey.

'If you don't mind, I'd like to go to the Venus Pool. It's a beautiful little beach where my son likes fishing.

Hopefully we'll see him.'

As they arrived at a small beach, they saw a tall boy wearing jeans, a white T-shirt, a blue baseball hat and no shoes. He was sitting on a rock beside a pile of large silver fish.

'Hey, Fletcher!' called Richard. 'Any luck?'

'Yes! I caught six big ones!'

'Excellent! Do you want a ride?'

Without another word, the boy climbed down off the rock, picked up his fish, and ran over to the carriage.

'This is my son, Fletcher,' said Richard. 'And this is Imran, Rubel ... and, I'm sorry Rubel – I don't know your daughter's name!' he said to Fizza's mum.

'Fizza,' said her mum, 'Fizza McIntyre.'

'Do you hear that, Fletcher? This young lady is a McIntyre!'

'So?' said Fletcher rudely.

'Fletcher and Fizza! Two F. McIntyres!' laughed Richard. 'You two should get on really well.'

All the adults laughed as, without smiling, the boy sat down next to her. Fizza could feel her face burning with embarrassment. The boy kept his face hidden under his hat and held the fish in his arms. They made Fizza feel even sicker. She even hated the smell of fish. Then she noticed that he didn't have a fishing rod or even a net.

'Where's your fishing rod?' she asked.

'I don't have one,' he said, without looking at her.

'Oh? So how did you catch them?' she asked.

Fletcher just held his dirty hands up in front of her and then turned his back on her.

'He caught those fish with his hands? I don't think so!' thought Fizza, taking an immediate dislike to this rude boy. And they didn't speak again for the rest of the journey.

* * *

Later, after supper, Fizza was practising her judo outside the cottage when she noticed a dark shape coming down the hill. As it got closer, she realised it was a black and white horse which was being ridden very quickly. She jumped out of the way to let it pass. Although the animal was so close she could hear its heavy breath, she couldn't see who the rider was because their face was covered by a green scarf.

Horses frightened Fizza – especially when they were going that fast.

'Stupid fool,' she said as she watched the dangerous rider disappear down the hill.

The next evening, after a pleasant day on the

beach, Fizza was practising her judo when she saw the black and white horse again. This time its rider had stopped it at the top of the field and they appeared to be looking down at the cottage. They remained like this for a few seconds before riding away. Fizza was in no doubt that it was the same horse and probably the same rider. But who was it?

On the third evening Fizza's mum and dad made plans for dinner.

'Fizza, we thought we'd go to the restaurant in the village tonight,' said her dad. 'Would you like that?'

Fizza had to think quickly. She didn't want to be away from the cottage. She didn't want to miss the mystery horse.

'Oh, thanks, but I'm feeling really tired this evening – I'd rather just have some soup and read my book.'

'Oh, we'll all stay here then!' said her mum.

'No, no – you go, I'll be fine,' replied Fizza quickly.

She said goodbye to her mum and dad, who promised to be home before it was dark, and went out into the field again to practise her judo moves. It was another beautiful evening, but after about an hour the sun began to set and Fizza began to feel tired. And this time there had been no sign of the black and white horse. She turned to go inside, but as she walked past the tree beside the cottage, one of the branches crashed down and somebody fell on top of her. Without thinking, she threw the person over her shoulder and onto the ground.

'Ow!'

It was a tall boy wearing jeans, a white T-shirt, no shoes and a blue baseball hat, which fell off to show thick red hair and a pair of the angriest green eyes Fizza had ever seen. It was Fletcher, Richard McIntyre's son!

'You!' said Fizza. 'Were you spying on me?'

'No!'

'Yes, you were! I saw you the other night too!'

Fletcher changed the subject. 'Anyway, you've broken my ankle!' he said, holding his leg.

'*I* broke your ankle? *You* were in the tree! You broke your own ankle!'

'Ow!' said Fletcher again.

Fizza suddenly felt a bit guilty for throwing him onto the ground.

'Do you think you can walk?' she asked a little more gently.

Fletcher shook his head.

'Here, put your arm round me. I'll help you to get up.'

With some difficulty, Fletcher stood up and Fizza helped him into the cottage where she sat him on a kitchen chair.

'Do you really think you've broken it?' she asked. 'Can you move it?'

She didn't know why she asked him that, but it was what people said in films.

'Yeah, a bit,' said Fletcher.

'Well, should I ask your dad to come and get you?'

'If you want,' he replied.

Fizza, annoyed by this boy's rudeness again, called his father on her mobile. By the time Richard McIntyre arrived, so had Fizza's mum and dad.

'What have you been doing, Fletcher?' laughed Richard.

'Nothing,' said Fletcher. 'I fell out of a tree, that's all. It's feeling better now.'

'Come on, let's get you home. Say thank you to Fizza,' Fletcher's dad said.

'Thanks,' said Fletcher quietly, as his dad helped him to leave the kitchen.

Through the window in the evening light, Fizza watched Richard McIntyre help Fletcher to get up onto a horse. There was no mistake. It was the black and white horse.

Chapter 5
The horses up the hill

The next morning Fizza was woken by a loud crash outside her bedroom window.

Rubbing her eyes, she looked at her watch. It said 12:15. How could she have slept for so long? Her thoughts were interrupted by more noise from outside.

'Oof!'

'Hup!'

'Oomph!'

It was the sound of two men fighting. Quickly she pulled back the curtain just in time to see her father throwing Richard McIntyre over his left shoulder.

'Ow!' cried Richard. 'My back!'

'You're still not landing correctly!' replied her dad. 'Let's try again.'

'Shouldn't we have a cup of coffee first, Imran?' asked Richard.

Fizza thought he sounded rather hopeful.

'No! Come on! You can do this!'

Fizza smiled to herself. Poor Richard! She knew how he must be feeling. Once her dad found a new judo student, he didn't let them escape easily.

A few moments later Fizza stepped out of the cottage and into the sunshine.

'Good morning, Fizza,' said her dad. 'Or should I say good afternoon?'

'Hello, Fizza,' said Richard, smiling up at her from his position on the grass.

'This Sark air makes you sleep deeply, doesn't it?'

It was true, she never slept so deeply at home.

'Yeah,' she said. 'Where's Fletcher today? How's his ankle?'

'Oh, his ankle's fine! He's driving one of my carriages for me so I've got the morning off—'

'And so I'm giving him some judo classes!' said her dad, putting out his hand to pull poor Richard back onto his feet.

'But I could tell him that you're hoping to see him!' continued Richard.

'Who?' said Fizza.

'Fletcher!'

'No, it's OK!' said Fizza quickly, but it was too late. Richard had already taken his mobile phone from his pocket.

'Fletcher! Is everything OK?' he shouted into the phone.

As Richard listened to his son's answer, Fizza tried to stop herself from screaming and running down the hill. Why did all adults have to embarrass her all the time? She didn't want to see that rude boy!

'Guess what, Fletcher!' Richard continued. 'I'm here with Fizza McIntyre at the cottage. Why don't you come over when you've finished?'

Poor Fizza thought she was going to explode with embarrassment, just like the time she saw Billy Adams in the Bullring Shopping Centre.

'And you must both stay for lunch!' said her mum, coming out of the cottage carrying two mugs of coffee.

'Could this get any worse?' thought Fizza.

At lunch the three adults talked happily but Fizza and Fletcher, who were sitting side by side, sat quietly without looking at one another.

'Thank you, Rubel! That was a delicious fish curry!' said Richard as he put down his knife and fork.

'Thank you,' said Fizza's mum. 'It's Fizza's favourite, isn't it, darling?'

Fizza made such a horrible face that it made Fletcher laugh out loud.

'At least he finds some things funny,' she thought.

'Thank you so much for lunch,' said Richard. 'Now I wonder if I could—'

Before he could finish his sentence, Fizza's dad had jumped up from the table.

'Do some more judo?'

'Uh, thanks, Imran,' said Richard, 'but I have another suggestion. Would you like to come and visit a friend who lives on the other side of the island? She makes beautiful pots.'

'How wonderful!' said Fizza's mum.

'I'd rather do some more judo,' said her dad.

'Imran!' said Rubel crossly. 'We'd love to, thank you Richard. What about you, Fizza?'

Fizza wanted to say that she would rather eat fish curry than go and visit a pot-maker, but, being a polite girl, she kept quiet.

'Perhaps Fizza would like to stay behind with Fletcher?' said Richard.

Fizza could feel her face turning red again.

'Fletcher,' he said, 'why don't you introduce Fizza to our horses?'

Fizza thought it would also be a bit rude if she said she didn't like horses.

'If she wants,' said Fletcher, without looking at her.

* * *

The two fifteen-year-olds watched as Richard McIntyre drove Rubel and Imran McIntyre in his horse and carriage along the coast road into the distance. Eventually the carriage disappeared from view, but they remained standing in silence. Fizza was beginning to wonder if they were going to stay like that all afternoon.

'So do you want to see the horses or not?' said Fletcher suddenly.

Fizza turned to face him and for the first time they looked at one another properly.

She could see a boy who had wide green eyes and little brown freckles on his nose and he could see a girl with warm, kind eyes and thick black hair that curled round her pretty face. At exactly the same moment, they smiled at one another.

'Yes, that would be great,' replied Fizza.

'Come on, we keep all the horses in the stables just up the hill. Are you OK walking?'

‘Of course I am!’ replied Fizza.

‘Oh yeah, I forgot. You are quite good at sport – for a girl.’

‘Thanks. And you’re quite good at riding – for a boy,’ Fizza replied and they ran up the hill together, laughing.

As they walked into a square yard, Fizza looked around her. She could see a line of wooden stables and in each stable there was a large horse.

‘Watch this,’ said Fletcher and he put his lips together and whistled.

Immediately the horses put their ears up and became very excited. They were obviously pleased to see him. However, Fizza moved behind Fletcher because they made her feel nervous.

‘It’s OK, Fizza, they won’t hurt you – they’re very gentle,’ said Fletcher. ‘These horses have to be large because they pull the carriages. We have three others who are still out working today.’

He put his hand on one of the horses and gently stroked it. Fizza could see that Fletcher loved these horses. Suddenly there was a loud noise behind them. It was the black and white horse and he was kicking his stable door.

'And that's Golden – he recognises you! He's saying hello!' laughed Fletcher.

'Golden?' replied Fizza. 'But he's not golden; he's black and white!'

'Yeah, but don't tell him, he doesn't know that!' he whispered.

Fizza laughed and then pointed at a pretty white horse that had a pink and grey nose.

'Don't tell me – that one's called Chocolate!' she said.

'Don't be silly – that's Cloudy! Why don't you give her a stroke?'

Very carefully Fizza put out her hand and stroked Cloudy's nose. She was surprised how soft it was.

'She's lovely,' said Fizza, relaxing a bit.

'Do you want to ride her?' said Fletcher.

Fizza immediately pulled her hand away. She had never ridden a horse before.

'Oh no! Thank you! No, I couldn't! I can't!'

Fletcher smiled at her.

'Come on, Fizza,' he said. 'Let me teach you.'

Chapter 6
The Country Cowboy

Fizza was standing in the middle of a field. Cloudy was on one side of her and Golden was on the other.

'Right,' said Fletcher. 'First! You have to get on – like this!'

And with a simple little jump, he climbed onto Golden.

'Now, you try.'

Nervously, Fizza held onto Cloudy's leather straps and kicked her leg high in the air – unfortunately, at that moment, Cloudy moved and Fizza fell to the ground. Fletcher laughed and laughed. It looked like he was going to fall off his horse.

'No, no, no! You're not *fighting* with her!' he laughed as, with tears in his eyes, he got off Golden.

'Here, let me help you,' he said, putting out his hand to help her get up.

Fizza was a bit cross at being laughed at and refused to take it at first.

'Oh, come on!' he said. 'Hold the saddle, give me your left leg ... and now lift your right leg up and over ... whoa! Look out!'

Fizza just missed Fletcher's head as she put her leg in the air, but the next thing she knew, she was sitting on top of Cloudy. Fletcher quickly jumped back on Golden.

'OK! Now!' he said. 'Let's go!'

He gave Golden a little kick and they took off across the field very quickly. Fizza's mouth dropped open as she watched them go.

'Is he crazy? I can't do that!' she thought.

However, as Fletcher reached the edge of the field, he turned Golden round and came back to her.

'Why didn't you follow me?' he said, laughing.

Fizza shook her head at him. This guy was crazy ... but he was OK.

'I'm not like you! I can't ride like a cowboy!' she said.

'I can't believe you've never ridden before. So what do you do in Birmingham?'

'I spend my time on my computer, I practise judo and I go to the shops at the Bullring sometimes.'

'The Bullring?'

'It's a shopping centre.'

'Do you like shopping?'

'Not really, but my friend Babs does.'

'Oh, I see,' said Fletcher, who couldn't understand why anyone would want to go shopping unless it was for horse food.

'Every cowboy needs a name,' he said, 'and so I'm going to call you ... the Bullring Kid!'

For the next two hours Fletcher McIntyre patiently taught Fizza McIntyre how to ride a horse. They started by walking the horses slowly and, little by little, he got Fizza to go a little faster. Once, when Cloudy went a bit too fast, Fizza became very frightened.

'I can't stop!' she cried out. 'I can't stop!'

Quickly, Fletcher chased after her, took Cloudy's straps and stopped her. He could see that she was crying.

'It's OK, it's OK, Fizza,' he said kindly, 'you're doing really well – I won't let you get hurt. I promise.'

And Fletcher kept his promise. Very gently and very patiently, he taught Fizza how to ride. By the end of the afternoon her bottom hurt a bit – but she'd had a brilliant time.

'Thank you,' she said as they led the horses back to the stables.

'No problem,' replied Fletcher. 'Um ... what are you doing tomorrow?'

'No plans,' said Fizza, suddenly shy. 'Why?'

'Well – would you like me to show you some of the island's secrets?'

'Can we go by horse?'

'Is there any other way?' Fletcher replied.

'It's a date!'

As soon as she said it, she realised that she shouldn't have used the word 'date'.

'I mean, that will be great!' she said quickly, feeling her face go red. She noticed that Fletcher's face was red too.

'OK,' he said. 'See you tomorrow.'

As Fizza made her way back to the cottage she realised that she hadn't thought of Birmingham or Babs or Billy Adams once all day.

* * *

During the next week Fizza and Fletcher went everywhere together. He showed her how to catch fish with her hands and she showed him her best judo moves. He showed her where the most amazing fish liked to swim and she showed him some clever tricks on his father's very old word processor. They climbed trees and swam in the beautiful clear waters of the Venus Pool. As they explored the island on their horses, Fizza got better and better at riding and she fell in love with Cloudy, the little white horse. Birmingham seemed light years away and they didn't talk about anything else apart from the island ... and the fact that their parents all seemed to be getting on so well. Richard had become Rubel and Imran's tour guide, Rubel had become Richard's cook and Imran had become Richard's judo teacher – whether Richard liked it or not! Fizza didn't know anything about Fletcher's mother. He only mentioned her once, when they were throwing stones into the sea.

'I haven't seen Dad enjoy himself so much in years – certainly not since Mum left,' he said.

'How long ago was that?' asked Fizza.

'Too long,' said Fletcher, as he threw a stone angrily into the waves.

Fizza could tell that he didn't want to talk about it, so she changed the subject.

'Well you can thank your dad, because my parents are having a lovely holiday ... and so am I!'

Fletcher smiled at her and jumped up.

'Last one in the sea's a bad egg!' he said.

And Fizza chased him into the sea still wearing her jeans.

* * *

One afternoon they explored a dark cave. At first Fizza couldn't see anything, but after a time she began to see things flying around above them.

'What are they?' she asked.

'Bats,' said Fletcher. 'They live in the dark.'

'Urgh! I hate bats,' said Fizza just as a small black bat flew straight at her head. She screamed loudly, which frightened the bat and it got caught in her hair.

'Agh! Get it off me! Get it off!' she cried.

'Hey! The Bullring Kid can't be afraid of bats – she's much too brave for that!' said Fletcher, laughing.

As he gently put out a hand and picked the bat out of Fizza's hair, the bat immediately became quiet, as if it felt safe in Fletcher's hand. Fizza decided that it was time to leave the cave.

'I think it's time for ice cream,' she said.

'All cowboys need ice cream!' said Fletcher.

Laughing, they climbed out of the cave and went to untie the horses, which were waiting patiently outside.

Later they sat on the harbour wall eating their ice creams.

'How do you do that?' asked Fizza.

'Do what?' replied Fletcher through a mouthful of strawberry ice cream.

'How do you get the animals to trust you?'

'I don't know; it just happens.'

At that moment a group of 'cool' girls walked past. They were the same girls Fizza had seen on the first day of her holiday. They looked at Fletcher and then at Fizza, whispered to one another and disappeared round the corner.

'Do you know them?' asked Fizza.

'Not really. They're in my class at school.'

He paused.

'They think I'm strange.'

'Why?' asked Fizza.

She suddenly realised that she didn't know anything about Fletcher's school or any of his friends.

'Because I'm different, I suppose. Actually, they call me the Country Cowboy.'

'Do you like that?' asked Fizza.

'I don't care really. The conversations I have with animals are much more interesting than talking about the stuff they all talk about ... but I like *some* people,' he added, looking shyly at her.

Fizza could feel herself turning red again.

'I don't think you can always trust people,' he said. 'But you can always trust animals.'

'Even crazy bats?'

'Even crazy bats!'

At that moment his phone rang.

'Hi, Dad!'

His smile quickly disappeared as he listened to his father.

'What? Are you sure? ... OK, I'll be right there.'

As he put his phone back into his pocket he turned to Fizza. His bright green eyes were now dark with anger.

'What did I say about not trusting people?'

'What's wrong, Fletcher?' asked Fizza.

'Two of the horses have been stolen.'

Chapter 7
Fizza has a plan

'I can't believe it,' said Richard McIntyre. 'This has never happened before.'

Fizza and Fletcher stood beside him. They all stared at the two empty stables.

'Who would steal them, Dad? Who's got them?' asked Fletcher angrily.

'Surely they can't be far away?' said Fizza. 'Sark's only a small place.'

'That's if they're still on the island,' said Fletcher.

'Well, you have called the police, haven't you?' said Fizza. 'They must search the island immediately!'

'Fizza! This isn't Birmingham!' said Fletcher sharply.

'What Fletcher means is that we only have one part-time officer on the island,' interrupted Richard gently.

'Oh, I see,' said Fizza.

'And where is he?' asked Fletcher.

'When I called him, he was out fishing – but he's coming back,' replied Richard.

Later they heard that other horses had been stolen on the larger islands of Guernsey and Jersey. The Sark policeman arrived at the stables, talked to Richard quietly for a few moments, and then called the Guernsey police for help.

'Unfortunately,' he said when he finished speaking to them, 'they are very busy at present, but they promise they will send help as soon as they can.'

This was too much for Fletcher, who kicked one of the stable doors angrily.

'That's not good enough!' he shouted.

'Son, we've got to be patient,' said Richard.

As Fletcher walked out of the yard, Richard looked at Fizza's worried face.

'It's OK, Fizza,' he said. 'Fletcher doesn't mean it. It's just that he loves these horses – perhaps even more than I do. They're more than our business to him – they're his family.'

At that moment Fizza's mum and dad arrived. Her dad was carrying a large saucepan.

'I thought everyone would like some food,' said Rubel. 'So I've made you all a fish curry!'

'And just when I thought things couldn't get any worse,' said Fizza under her breath.

For the first time that afternoon, Richard McIntyre laughed.

* * *

Fizza found Fletcher sitting on a wall, looking down the hill and out to sea, and she sat down next to him. Together, they watched the sun turn from a deep orange to blood red as it dropped out of the sky. Eventually Fletcher made a little noise, which made Fizza turn to look at him. His face was wet with tears.

'Fletcher,' she said. 'It's going to be OK. I know it is.'

'No, it's not!' he said angrily. 'It never is! I'm fed up with having things taken away from me!'

'You'll get the horses back, I know you will.'

'*She* never came back.'

'Who?' Fizza asked.

'Her.'

He looked down at his hands.

'Mum.'

Fizza looked out to sea. She didn't really know what to say. She'd always had a mum there for her – she didn't know what it was like not to have a mum. So she decided to keep quiet and listen as Fletcher began to talk. He told Fizza how one day, at the age of ten, he came home from school and found his father crying at the kitchen table. In his large hands he held a note from his wife, Fletcher's mother. It said that she couldn't stay any more. She needed a life away from Sark. She needed a life. And that was that. That morning, Fletcher had seen her for the last time. His parents eventually divorced and so, for the past five years, it had been just him and his dad ... and the horses.

'I've never spoken to anyone about it before,' he said. 'I've never wanted to.'

Fizza looked at him and gave him a little smile. She suddenly felt closer to Fletcher than she had felt to any of her friends, even Babs.

'Thanks,' he said, cleaning the tears from his face with his T-shirt.

'Any time,' said Fizza.

They smiled at one another and looked out to sea again.

'Right!' said Fizza suddenly. 'We have to get some horses back! And guess what?'

Fletcher sat up and looked at her with his wide, wet green eyes.

'What?' he said.

'I've got a plan.'

* * *

The two fifteen-year-olds led Cloudy into the middle of the field under the dark midnight sky. The little horse's white coat shone under the light of the moon.

'It's OK, girl!' whispered Fletcher into her ear as he tied her to a small tree. 'We'll watch you!'

Quickly they moved back into the dark corner of the field and left the horse standing alone.

'I can't look at her! She looks so frightened!' said Fizza. She was beginning to wish that she hadn't had the idea of leaving a horse out as a trap to catch horse thieves.

However, Fletcher and Fizza hid themselves behind a large tree and watched Cloudy. They had chosen her for this job because of her bright white coat which could easily be seen from a few hundred metres away. An hour went past and nothing happened, and then another. Fizza was getting tired and her eyes were becoming heavy.

'Fletcher!' she whispered. 'Shall we just give up? This is silly! It's obvious no one's coming to take her!'

Suddenly Fletcher took hold of her arm.

'Shh!' he said. 'Look! What's that?'

On the far side of the field, they could see a small light and Fizza held her breath as it moved towards the little white shape of Cloudy. Soon, they could both see that the light was being carried by a man.

'This is it!' whispered Fletcher.

After a few moments, the man got to the horse and as quickly as he had appeared, he disappeared into the darkness, taking the little horse with him.

'Poor Cloudy!' said Fizza.

'Come on!' Fletcher whispered as he ran forward to follow them.

As they came to the far edge of the field they looked down the hill towards the moonlit sea. At first they couldn't see anything, but then suddenly Fizza jumped.

'There she is!' she said.

Fletcher looked down the hill and saw, moving along quite slowly, the unmistakable white shape of Cloudy.

'Come on!' he whispered. 'But keep your distance!'

Slowly and as quietly as they could, they followed the horse and her kidnapper for about twenty minutes. They couldn't see where they were going and several times they fell against rocks and bushes. Fizza's feet were beginning to hurt and she was cold. She wished she'd put a warmer sweater on. The sea was on their right but it became hidden when they passed behind some tall trees.

'I think he's taking her down to Derrible Bay,' said Fletcher.

They knew the sea was near because they could hear the waves crashing onto a beach. Now Fizza was worried because she hadn't planned what to do next if her plan worked!

'So now what are we supposed to do?' she whispered to Fletcher in the dark.

'It's OK, Fizza,' he said. 'This time it's *my* turn to have the plan.'

And he took his phone out of his pocket.

Chapter 8
Laying a trap

Fletcher and Fizza climbed quietly down the hill a few more metres and looked out carefully from behind a small bush. Cloudy's kidnapper was talking to another man who he had met on the beach. The men were so close that Fizza and Fletcher could hear them speak. In the dark they could see that one was fat and the other one was thin. It was the thin one that had stolen Cloudy.

'Well done! That looks like a nice horse!' the fat man said.

'Yes, we should get a good price for it,' replied the thin man. 'When's the boat going to get here?'

'Any moment now ... I'll get the others,' said the fat man.

He disappeared behind some big rocks in a corner of the beach. After a few seconds he came back out of the dark. He was leading two large horses.

'They're our horses!' whispered Fletcher angrily. 'Those men have been keeping them here!'

The men were obviously waiting for a boat which

would get them off the island. A few moments later a green light flashed three times out at sea.

'Hey! That's the sign! They're here!' the thin man shouted.

Fizza and Fletcher realised that if they were going to stop these men, they had to act now before help arrived.

'OK, Fizza,' whispered Fletcher, 'this is what we've got to do ...'

Seconds later Fizza waited in her position while Fletcher gave a low whistle. All three horses on the sand put their heads up and listened, but the men didn't notice anything. They were too busy looking for their boat. Then Fletcher whistled again and the horses began to jump in excitement. This *did* surprise the men. Every time Fletcher whistled, the horses jumped until they managed to pull their ropes free from the men's hands. Then they began to run in circles around them.

'Catch them, stupid!' shouted one of the men.

'You try! They're too quick!' replied the other one.

This was the moment Fizza was waiting for. She ran onto the beach, jumped in the air, gave a high kick and knocked the fat man down to the ground.

'Oi!' shouted the thin man. He tried to run and help his friend, but all three horses moved into his way. He couldn't move! Fizza sat on top of the fat man, who lay face down, and held his arms behind his back.

'Ow! That hurts!' he cried.

'Well, don't move then!' replied Fizza.

She watched as Fletcher tied the thin man's hands and feet together with a rope and then she looked out to sea. The lights from the kidnappers' boat were getting much nearer, making the horses run away.

'What are we going to do when that boat gets here?' she asked Fletcher.

'Yeah!' said the fat man through a mouthful of sand. 'What *are* you going to do?'

'It's OK,' said Fletcher. 'It's going to be OK.'

In truth, Fletcher was beginning to get a bit worried too. However, just at that moment they heard a familiar voice.

'Fletcher? Is that you?'

'Dad!'

Richard McIntyre appeared out of the dark. Behind him was Fizza's dad, Imran, and, farther back, two of his carriage drivers.

'There you are!' said Fletcher. 'I was beginning to think that you hadn't gotten my message to meet me here!'

Fizza looked at her own father in surprise.

'Dad?' said Fizza. 'What are you doing here?'

'I thought you might need some help,' replied her father, looking at the helpless fat man, 'but now I see that you did learn something from my classes after all!'

'So you've found the horses!' said Richard. 'Well done!'

Then he looked serious.

'Fletcher, why didn't you tell me what you were doing?' he said. 'These men could be dangerous!'

The thin man nodded his head in agreement, but everyone ignored him.

'It's OK, Dad. Fizza and I had it under control, didn't we, Fizz?'

As Fizza smiled, she noticed that the kidnappers' boat was really close now. She still wasn't sure what was going to happen when it arrived. There could be lots more men! However, just as it arrived at the beach, the boat was flooded with a very bright light.

'Stop! This is the police! Turn off your engine!' a voice shouted through a loudspeaker.

The bright light came from four police boats which had arrived very quietly in the dark water and completely surprised the kidnappers. The police boats made a circle round them and they had no way of escape.

'It looks like our Sark policeman asked his friends from Guernsey to come,' said Richard. 'He said he would when I called him.'

'Fizza looked at Fletcher and smiled.

'OK, Country Cowboy?'

'Not bad, Bullring Kid,' he replied. 'Not bad.'

* * *

The next day was a good day and a bad one. It was good because Fizza and Fletcher had helped catch the horse thieves. And this had made them local heroes. However, it was bad because it was the last day of Fizza's holiday. It was almost a joke – two weeks ago she hadn't wanted to come to Sark and now she didn't want to leave it!

Richard McIntyre took them to the harbour with their suitcases. She watched sadly as he unloaded their suitcases from his carriage onto the road. As Imran said goodbye, he promised Richard free judo classes if he came to Birmingham. Then Richard kissed Rubel on the cheek and thanked her for her wonderful fish curry. Then it was Fizza's turn to say goodbye to Fletcher who was sitting on a wall.

'Say goodbye to the horses for me,' she said because she didn't want to say goodbye to him. 'It's been great. Thanks.'

'Yeah,' said Fletcher quietly without looking at her, 'the best.'

Suddenly shy, Fizza climbed sadly onto the boat. But when she turned back, he had gone. And she knew she would probably never see him again.

'He doesn't care I'm going!' she thought. 'He didn't even wait for the boat to leave!'

But Fizza McIntyre didn't know the real reason. Fletcher McIntyre had left because, once again, someone was leaving him behind. And that person had become very special to him.

As the boat began its journey across the sea, Fizza's mum and dad waved at Richard until he disappeared from view. Then Fizza's mum turned and smiled at Fizza.

'Do you know something, Fizza?' she said.

Fizza was too miserable to reply at first.

'I think The Richard McIntyre Horse and Carriage Company could be the answer to some of Birmingham's big problems.'

'What do you mean?' asked Fizza, staring at the waves.

'Wait and see, Fizza. Wait and see.'

Chapter 9
Fizza takes the blame

It was the first day of the autumn term and Fizza walked slowly through the school gates.

'Fizza!'

She turned and saw her friend Babs running towards her.

'Fizza! Guess what!'

'What?' said Fizza.

'I'm in love!'

'With Billy?'

'Billy who?' said Babs. 'No! It's a wonderful boy I met in Greece. He's called Jake and he's really good-looking! I'm crazy about him!'

And Babs told Fizza all about Jake and where he was from and how they planned to see each other again soon.

'And how was your holiday, Fizza?' she said when she had eventually finished. 'How was Sark?'

'Cool,' said Fizza. 'It was cool.'

At that moment Babs's mobile phone made a sound.

'Oh!' cried Babs. 'It's a text from Jake! Excuse me!'

Fizza smiled. Last term Babs was madly in love with Billy Adams. This term, however, she had forgotten who he was and she was madly in love with someone else.

* * *

Fizza had a surprise that morning and it wasn't a good one. The whole school was in the large hall to hear the headmaster speak. All the children listened and tried not to yawn, as he talked and talked.

'Now, I have something very serious to say about some very bad behaviour last term.'

Everyone sat up and listened.

'At the end of last term certain students were responsible for this.'

He held up a photograph of two of the teachers. One lady teacher had a beard and was wearing men's trousers and beside her was a man wearing a dress covered in yellow flowers. Fizza recognised it immediately. It was one of the photos she had changed for Billy Adams.

'Nobody will be able to use the computer rooms

until the person – or people – who did this come and see me in my office,' said the headmaster. 'Now, all go to your classes, please.'

Fizza couldn't move. It was her! Babs looked at her with wide eyes and she could feel the 'cool' girls whispering behind her.

'What are you going to do?' whispered Babs.

Fizza knew what she had to do.

'I have to go and see the headmaster,' she said.

'But what about Billy Adams? It was his idea!' said Babs.

'But *I* did it,' said Fizza. 'See you later.'

And she left the school hall and went to wait outside the headmaster's office.

*　　*　　*

The headmaster looked at Fizza over the top of his glasses. He had Fizza's photographs of the teachers on his desk.

'This is most unlike you, Felicity. Why did you do it?'

'I don't know. I thought it was a funny thing to do, I suppose.'

The headmaster shook his head. He was obviously surprised.

'And you did it all on your own?'

Fizza paused. She was not going to give Billy Adams's name, even if it had been his idea.

'Yes, sir,' she said, trying not to cry.

'Well, in that case—' began the headmaster, but he was interrupted by a knock on the door.

It was the school secretary.

'I have Billy Adams here. He would like to see you.'

As Billy Adams walked into the office, Fizza realised she hadn't seen him since that day in the Bullring Shopping Centre in the holidays. He had a suntan from the summer sunshine and his blond hair was longer and almost white now. Fizza thought he looked more handsome than ever.

'Hello, Billy, can I help you?' asked the headmaster.

'Sir, it was my idea,' he said. 'The computer trick was all my idea.'

He stood looking straight ahead without once looking at Fizza.

'But,' the headmaster said, 'Felicity said she did it all on her own.'

'Well, she's wrong, sir. It was my idea,' replied Billy.

'What a great guy,' thought Fizza. 'He's taking the blame for the whole thing!'

The truth was that Billy Adams felt guilty. The joke on the teachers had been his idea and it wasn't fair if this quiet girl got into trouble for it. The headmaster listened as Billy explained what had happened.

'Billy, I understand that it was your idea, but Felicity shouldn't have helped you,' said the headmaster. 'It was wrong of both of you.'

However, secretly the headmaster was pleased with their honesty. He told them to write a letter of apology to all the teachers in the photographs.

'Now, go back to your classes and if there is any more bad behaviour this term, you'll be in trouble.'

Outside in the corridor, Fizza was just about to walk away, but Billy stopped her.

'Thank you,' he said. 'You didn't need to take the blame.'

'Yes, I did,' said Fizza. 'I did it, too.'

Billy took a closer look at Fizza. He couldn't believe that this was the same girl who had helped him with the photos at the end of the last term. She was so different! She was so confident! And he hadn't realised she was so pretty!

*　*　*

Fizza's mum was waiting for her in the kitchen when she got home from school. She looked serious.

'Hello, Fizza,' she said. 'I had a phone call today ...'

'Oh no,' thought Fizza. 'It must have been the headmaster! Now Mum's going to be cross with me!'

'And I have to say—' said her mum.

Fizza waited to be told off.

'—that something very exciting is going to happen in Birmingham soon! But it's got to be a secret! I can't tell you until it's final!'

And then her mum jumped around the kitchen in excitement.

'What is it?' asked Fizza, laughing.

'Oh, I can't tell you! I wish I could, but it's Council business! And all things have to be done correctly.'

'Can't you tell me anything?' asked Fizza.

'OK,' said her mum. 'I'll say two words: "horses" and "carriages"!'

And it didn't matter how many questions Fizza asked her mum, she wouldn't tell her any more.

'Anyway,' she said, changing the subject. 'How was your first day back at school?'

Fizza was just wondering if she should tell her

mum about getting into trouble with the headmaster when the phone rang.

'I'll get it!' she said as she ran for the phone.

'Hello?' she said.

'Is that Fizza?' a boy's voice said.

'Yes?'

'Fizza, it's Billy. Billy Adams.'

Fizza's heart gave a little jump.

'Oh, hello,' she said, trying her best to sound cool.

'I wondered if you'd like to come to the park.'

'When?'

'This evening?'

An hour later Fizza found herself walking through the park with Billy Adams. What a crazy day it had been! She had started the day feeling really miserable and she was ending the day feeling wonderful! As they walked, they talked about school, family and friends. He told her how he loved football and playing his guitar and she told him about her judo.

'Show me a move then!' said Billy.

And so Fizza threw him over her back and onto the ground and this made them laugh a lot.

'Where did you learn to do that?' he said as he lay on the grass.

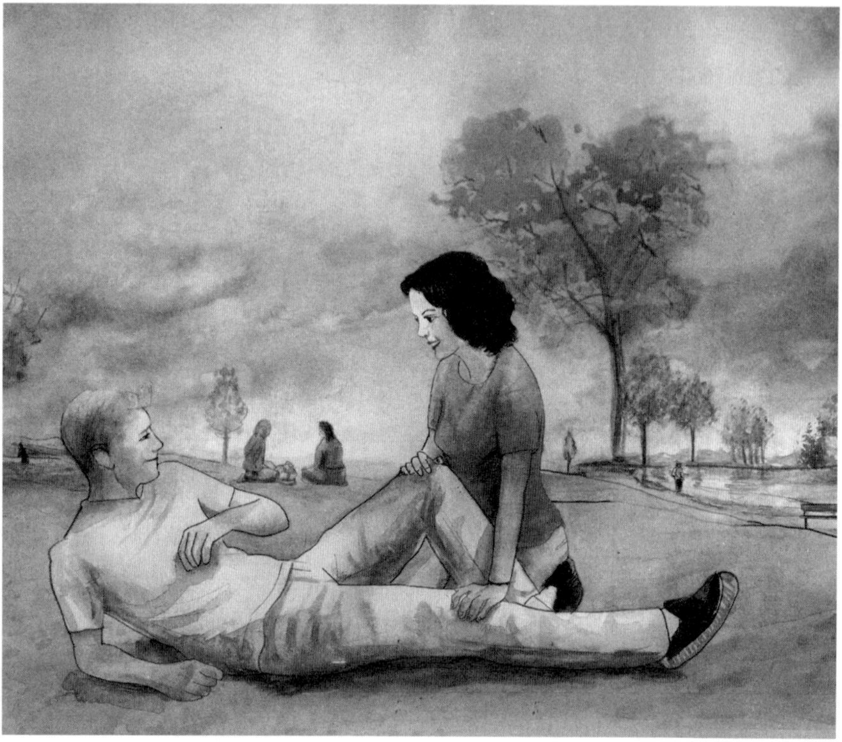

'My dad taught me!' laughed Fizza.

'Well, tell him I want some classes!'

Then they began to talk about their holidays in the summer and Fizza told him all about her adventures on Sark, the horses and Fletcher.

'So was it a holiday romance?' asked Billy.

Fizza laughed.

'No! Of course not! He was just a really good friend!'

As it began to get dark, Billy walked her home.

'Would you like to do this again?' he asked her as they stood outside her house.

'Yes. That would be nice,' she replied.

'What about tomorrow evening? Are you free?'

'Yes. I'm free,' she said.

Suddenly her holiday on Sark seemed like a very long time ago.

Chapter 10
A new student

Two weeks later Fizza walked through the school gates.

'Fizza!'

She turned and saw Babs running towards her.

'Fizza! Is it true?'

'Is what true?'

'Are you going out with Billy Adams?'

Fizza laughed.

'What? No! Of course not! He's just a friend.'

'Hmm,' said Babs.

It was obvious Babs didn't believe her.

In the fortnight since the beginning of term, Fizza had spent quite a lot of time with Billy. They had been to the park and the cinema, and he'd even been to her house and her dad had taught him some judo moves. But they hadn't held hands or kissed! She wasn't shy of him any more, but they weren't girlfriend and boyfriend, they were just friends.

'You know everyone at school is talking about you?' said Babs.

Fizza did know. She had noticed the 'cool' girls whispering about her, but she had tried to ignore them.

'Let them talk!' laughed Fizza.

But Babs didn't laugh because, although she had met Jake on holiday, she was a bit jealous of Fizza's relationship with Billy. After all, she had said that she liked him first!

* * *

Fizza was late to class because she had to take some books back to the library. As she walked through the classroom door, she stopped in surprise because, sitting at one of the front desks, was a red-haired boy with green eyes and freckles. It was Fletcher McIntyre.

'Hello, Fizza,' he said.

At first Fizza couldn't speak. She just stood with her mouth open. This must have been her mum's 'secret'!

'Fletcher?' she said. 'What are you doing here?'

Immediately, all the 'cool' girls began to whisper. Then the teacher told Fizza to sit down and class began.

At break time Fizza and Fletcher sat in a corner of the playground so that they could talk. Fletcher explained that his dad had been offered a job by Birmingham City Council.

'You mean my mum offered him a job!' said Fizza.

'I guess so,' said Fletcher.

'What is it?'

'It's a "green" taxi service,' he explained. 'He's brought the horses and carriages from Sark.'

Fizza had a hundred questions.

'Where are you living? Is Cloudy here? Where are the horses?'

Fletcher explained that his father had rented a house and stables in Birmingham.

'We were really lucky to get it,' he said. 'Apparently there's a man with a factory next door who also wants the land. He wants to build on it, or something.'

'So you've brought the countryside to the city!' laughed Fizza. 'Well, you showed me the secrets of Sark; now it's my turn to show you the secrets of this school!'

And so that morning Fizza took Fletcher around the school and his wide green eyes grew even wider as she showed him all the different classrooms and corridors. She watched him as he stared everywhere in astonishment, and she laughed as he ran out of the way to let the crowds of students pass as they went from class to class.

'There are more people in this school than on the whole of Sark!' he whispered.

Fizza introduced Fletcher to her friends. She told them that he knew more about the countryside and animals than anyone else she knew. He was amazing! However, not everyone felt the same as Fizza.

'Who is he?' whispered Babs, thinking that he needed a good haircut.

'He's my friend from Sark!' said Fizza.

'Isn't he a bit ...'

'What?'

'You know ... strange,' said Babs. 'He jumps every time an ambulance goes past the school!'

'You don't know him!' said Fizza.

'And where did he get those shoes? They're awful!'

'Oh, do shut up, Babs!'

Fizza thought of how he rode horses, caught fish with his hands and climbed the highest trees. Babs didn't know how wonderful Fletcher was, because she hadn't seen him do these things!

As the bell rang for the end of school, Fletcher asked Fizza if she wanted to come and see the horses that evening.

'I'd love to!' said Fizza.

Richard McIntyre was waiting to collect Fletcher at the school gates and he waved at Fizza. Fizza thought it was such fun to see a horse and carriage outside the school!

'See you later!' said Fletcher as he ran happily over to his dad and climbed up on the carriage. Fizza suddenly realised that other students were laughing at him. Some girls from her class, including Babs, walked past her.

'Is "horse boy" your brother?' asked one.

'No, why?' said Fizza.

'Well, you're both called McIntyre.'

Fizza didn't answer.

'I think he's her boyfriend!' said Babs and they all laughed and walked away.

Fizza watched them go. What was wrong with Babs? Why was she being so unkind too?

* * *

Later, just as Fizza was getting ready to go to see Fletcher and the horses at the stables, the bell rang. Fizza answered the door and found Billy standing on the step.

'Hi, Fizza. Are you ready?' he said.

'Am I ready for what?'

'The cinema! We arranged it last week! I've got the tickets!' he said.

'Oh yes! Of course!' lied Fizza. She had completely forgotten.

As she ran to get her coat, she hoped that Fletcher wouldn't mind if she didn't go to the stables that evening.

* * *

The next day Fizza felt extremely guilty as she ran into school. She saw Fletcher sitting in a corner of the playground reading a book.

'Fletcher! I'm so sorry I couldn't come to the stables last night. I had lots of homework,' she lied.

'It doesn't matter,' he said.

'Perhaps I could come tonight?'

'If you want to,' he said and he went back to reading his book.

Later, at break time, just as Fizza was trying to talk to Fletcher again, Billy came over.

'Hi, Fizza,' he said.

'Fletcher, this is Billy. Billy, this is Fletcher, from Sark,' she said.

'Hi, Fletcher,' said Billy.

But Fletcher ignored him and turned his head

away. Fizza looked at him. He was behaving just like he had the first time she had met him on Sark: rude, bad-tempered, *unlikeable*. Not like Billy. The previous evening she had had a lovely time with Billy at the cinema – as she always did.

'Wasn't that film last night funny?' said Billy.

Fletcher turned and stared angrily at Fizza. Now he knew the real reason why she had not gone to the stables. Fizza tried to smile at him, but he just walked towards a tree, climbed it and sat in the highest branch he could find.

'Is he OK?' asked Billy. 'He's a bit—'

'What?' replied Fizza sharply.

'You know ... strange?' said Billy, who didn't like Fizza's relationship with this odd boy. Why couldn't he go back to Sark?

'He's not strange!' said Fizza. 'He's great! He's just arrived here, that's all!'

By then other students had started laughing at the new red-haired boy who had climbed the tree. And they laughed even more when the school cat climbed up and sat with him.

'Poor Fletcher,' thought Fizza. 'I should have gone to see him last night! He doesn't know anyone in the whole of Birmingham! What sort of friend am I?'

At the end of the day, Fizza saw Fletcher walking out of the school gates. He didn't look very happy.

'Fletcher! Wait!'

But he carried on walking.

'Fletcher! I'll come over to the stables later, shall I?' she said as she ran along beside him.

'If you want, but don't you have a date with your boyfriend?' he said.

Suddenly Fizza realised that Fletcher was jealous.

'No, I don't and he's not my boyfriend, silly!' she replied just as Billy Adams walked past them.

'Hi, Fizza,' Billy said, making sure he had his back to Fletcher. 'What are you doing later?'

'It doesn't matter,' interrupted Fletcher.

'I wasn't talking to you, country boy!' Billy replied.

This was too much for Fletcher, who jumped on top of Billy and began to hit him as hard as he could. In return, Billy kicked him and before Fizza knew what was happening, the two boys were in a terrible fight.

'Stop it!' she said. 'Please!'

However, they continued to fight, so she took Billy's left arm, held it behind his back and pulled him away from Fletcher. Then she gave Fletcher one of her best kicks and knocked him to the ground.

'Ow!' said Billy.

'Oomph!' cried Fletcher.

'I said "Stop it!"' said Fizza as she walked away.

Why couldn't she like two boys at once? Surely she didn't have to choose? For months, years even, nothing had ever happened to Fizza McIntyre. Now everything was happening at once and she wasn't sure if she liked it.

Chapter 11
Bad neighbours and good friends

Fletcher and Fizza got off the bus in the centre of Birmingham. All around them were tall buildings and lorries, buses and cars that queued past them.

'Where are they, then?' Fizza shouted in an attempt to be heard over the noise of the traffic.

'What?'

'The stables! Where are they?'

'Over there!' shouted Fletcher, pointing at an ugly grey wall which had an old wooden gate in the centre of it. Fizza could just see the tops of the stables on the other side and a small stone house. Next door to the stables was a large factory with the words 'Scully's Waste' written in large red letters on its roof. Several of the factory's lorries were parked right next to it. Fizza was very much a city girl, but even she hadn't expected this. To her, stables should be in the middle of the country, just like they had been on Sark. It seemed crazy to find them in the middle of a city!

'You're joking!' she said. 'You must hate it here!'

'It's OK once you get inside,' said Fletcher. 'Come on. Oh, and please don't mention the fight – Dad will go crazy.'

'Only if you don't tell my mum that I joined in!' she replied. 'She's meeting me here.'

Smiling, Fletcher opened the large wooden gate and they stepped into the yard. He was right: once they were inside the wall it didn't feel that different from the stables on Sark. The first thing Fizza saw was a line of stables and in each stable there was a horse. They were the same kind faces that she had loved when she was on holiday on Sark and they all turned to say hello. Then Fizza heard someone kicking against a stable door.

'I know who that is!' she said.

And she had guessed right, because in a corner of the yard was a handsome black and white horse.

'Hello, Golden!' laughed Fizza as she went over to him. Then she saw Cloudy and ran over to her to stroke her nose.

'Oh! Cloudy! It's so good to see them all again!' she cried.

'Yeah. They think it's good to see you too,' said Fletcher.

At that moment Fletcher's dad came out of the house followed by Fizza's mum. They were both holding mugs of tea.

'It's Miss Fizza McIntyre! The judo kid who saved my horses!' he cried.

Fizza smiled. She really liked Fletcher's dad. He was always so happy.

'It's Mr Richard McIntyre! The man who's brought a little bit of Sark to Birmingham to make it greener!' she replied. 'How's the taxi service?'

'Well, it's only just started but hopefully it's going to be OK!' said Richard.

'I know it's going to be very successful!' said Fizza's mum. 'So how was school?'

'Great!' lied Fizza and Fletcher together.

'Have you made lots of new friends, Fletcher?' asked Richard.

Luckily, before Fletcher could answer his dad, he was interrupted by the loud noise of several engines. All of the Scully's Waste lorries had started up at once. Then the drivers began to sound their horns over and over again. For the first time ever, Fizza saw Richard McIntyre become angry.

'Why do they keep doing that?' he asked. 'It's the fourth time they've done it in an hour. They're frightening the horses!'

'I told you, Richard,' said Fizza's mum. 'It's Robert Scully. He owns the factory and he's annoyed the City Council has given this land to you and not to him. He likes getting what he wants! He's already complained to the Council. He'll relax, I'm sure.'

Cloudy was shaking her head. The poor horse didn't like the noise at all. Suddenly they saw a short man standing at the gate. He had grey hair combed back from his red face and wore a brown suit.

'Sorry, McIntyre. Are my lorries making too much noise?'

Fizza and Fletcher immediately knew who it was. It had to be Robert Scully.

'Well, they *are* frightening the horses—' began Richard.

'Sorry! My drivers can be very naughty sometimes!' replied Scully and he walked away, laughing.

Fizza and Fletcher looked at one another. They didn't like Robert Scully at all.

* * *

The next morning Fizza met Fletcher just as he got off the bus outside the school.

'Hi, Fizza,' he said.

'Hi, Fletcher. Did Robert Scully's lorries make any more noise last night?'

'No, but we heard them all go out early this morning.'

'Well, hopefully Mum's right – he'll relax soon.'

'Yeah, I hope so.'

As they walked through the gates, they saw Billy Adams coming in the opposite direction.

'Oh no, look who it is,' said Fletcher.

'Oh, Fletcher, can't you try to be friends with him?'

'I don't want to be his friend,' replied Fletcher.

'I think that you two would get on really well. He's OK really.'

Fletcher paused and looked at her.

'OK,' he said, 'I'll try. Just for you.'

Fizza smiled at Fletcher. She knew how difficult this must be for him, especially as he was the new boy. A few seconds later, as Billy Adams walked round the corner, Fletcher was waiting for him.

'Erm. Hi, Billy,' he began.

Billy stopped. He had a biscuit in his hand and he was chewing.

'Yeah?' he said.

'I just wanted to say that I'm sorry for fighting with you,' said Fletcher.

However, Fletcher realised that Billy wasn't looking at him because he was staring right past him. Fletcher was beginning to find it difficult to be patient.

'Look, Billy, I'm trying to be friendly here, but if you don't want to be ...'

Without saying another word, Billy began to run towards the school.

'I'm not that frightening, am I?' Fletcher asked an equally surprised Fizza.

At that moment, a big black dog ran past them. But it didn't run past Billy – it chased him.

'Do you think it's after Billy's biscuit?' asked Fizza.

'I don't know – whatever it is, it doesn't look very friendly!' said Fletcher as he dropped his bag and ran after the dog.

Billy jumped up onto a wall and ran along it but the angry dog ran along beside him. Billy was cornered. The dog stared up at him, showed its teeth and began to growl. It did not like poor frightened Billy at all.

'It's OK, Billy!' whispered Fletcher. 'Throw your

biscuit on the ground!'

Immediately, Billy threw the half-eaten biscuit onto the grass. The dog ate it, but still seemed to be interested in Billy.

By now a crowd of students had gathered and were watching in excitement. Very slowly Fletcher bent down and called softly to the dog.

'Here, boy!'

The dog turned and began to move towards Fletcher. For a moment it looked like it was going to attack him too.

'It's OK, boy, come here ...' said Fletcher gently.

Suddenly the dog dropped its ears, put its head down and walked over to Fletcher.

'Good boy!' said Fletcher, holding onto the dog. 'Good boy!'

As soon as he knew he was safe, Billy jumped off the wall.

'Thanks, Fletcher,' he said quietly.

'It's OK,' replied Fletcher.

Fizza came over to join them.

'Right,' she said. 'Let's start again, shall we?'

The two boys laughed.

'Billy, this is Fletcher. Fletcher, this is Billy,' she

said.

'Hi, Fletcher,' said Billy, smiling.

'Hi, nice to meet you, Billy,' replied Fletcher.

Chapter 12

A message for the McIntyres

Soon the story of Fletcher McIntyre saving Billy Adams from a mad dog was hot news all through the school. Fletcher became a hero.

Fizza watched happily as Fletcher joined Billy and his friends in a game of football.

Even Babs suddenly became very interested in Fletcher and she spent the whole maths class asking him about his horses.

'How interesting!' she said when he told her about his dad's new taxi service. 'I'd love to come and see them!'

Fizza listened to their conversation. Babs didn't even like horses! Then she heard some of the other girls talking about him.

'He's kind of handsome,' whispered one.

'Yeah,' replied her friend, 'but he'd be even better-looking if he wore better clothes!'

'Well, girls, should we take him shopping tonight?'

Babs called out to them.

'Yeah!'

'Is that OK with you, Fletcher?' asked Babs through her pretty long eyelashes.

'Er, yeah. Sure!' smiled Fletcher.

'Can we take one of your dad's taxis?'

'OK!'

At the end of the day, Fizza watched as Fletcher, Babs and two other girls climbed excitedly into one of Richard McIntyre's carriages. Babs hadn't even asked her if she wanted to join them! Fizza suddenly felt very lonely and realised that she was jealous. She didn't know if she was jealous of Babs, or if she was jealous that Fletcher was having a good time without her.

'It's not fair!' she thought. 'Fletcher McIntyre is *my* friend!'

As the carriage pulled away, Fletcher saw her standing by the school gate and stood up.

'Fizza! Aren't you coming?' he shouted.

'No, thanks! I've got better things to do!' she replied.

'She's got "better things to do", Fletcher!' said Babs in a silly voice as she pulled him back down.

Fizza couldn't believe that Babs was being so mean to her! Miserably, she watched the carriage full of silly laughing girls and Fletcher drive away. However, even before they'd disappeared from view, Fizza knew that she was being silly. She should be pleased that Fletcher was happy at school now.

'Stop being so selfish, Fizza McIntyre!' she said to herself.

She decided to go and see him at the stables later.

* * *

After tea, when Fizza arrived at the stables, she found the large gate in the wall had been left open. She stopped before she entered the yard.

'Hello! Is anyone in? It's me! Fizza!' she shouted.

As there was no reply, she gently pushed the gate open wide. She noticed that a few of the stables were empty and several of the carriages had gone.

'Richard's taxi service is having a busy day,' she thought.

Then she looked further into the yard. There was no sign of Fletcher, who was probably still out shopping with the girls. She smiled as she wondered if Fletcher was enjoying himself. Then suddenly she stopped smiling because she realised something was wrong. Something was very wrong. Quickly she looked around at all the stables and what she saw made her feel sick. A message had been written in red paint on every door.

'Get out!'

'Go back to Sark!'

'Leave ... or it's horse on the menu!'

Fizza put her hand to her mouth and stared at the words. This was horrible!

'Oh my goodness!' she thought. 'I hope the horses are OK!'

Quickly she ran from stable to stable and saw that Cloudy, Golden and the other horses were safe. Then she called Fletcher on her mobile phone. After a couple of rings he answered.

'Fizza! You should be here! They're trying to make me wear pink!' he laughed.

Fizza could hear girls' laughter behind him.

'Fletcher. You have to come back to the stables. Now!'

There was a pause.

'Why?' he asked, his voice suddenly serious.

Fizza took a deep breath.

'Someone's left you a message.'

*   *   *

The next day after school Fizza, Fletcher and Billy sat in her garden discussing what had happened at the stables.

'Dad's really upset,' said Fletcher.

'I'm not surprised! But he's not thinking of leaving Birmingham, is he?' asked Fizza.

'I don't know. He's worried that if it happens again, the horses could get hurt.'

'So, do you think it was Robert Scully?' asked Fizza.

'I don't think – I *know* it was Robert Scully – or one of his men,' said Fletcher.

'But the police say that there's nothing to show that it was him.'

'Scully's not a nice man,' said Billy. 'My dad used to be one of his drivers years ago.'

'I'd love to do something to Scully,' said Fizza.

They all sat and thought for a while.

'Shall we go and write messages on his lorries?' suggested Billy.

'No,' said Fizza. 'We can do better than that.'

'Oh, yeah?' said Fletcher.

Fizza nodded her head.

'What did your dad think of Scully, Billy?' she asked.

'He hated him. He thought that Scully had secrets – but Scully got rid of him before he could find out what they were,' replied Billy.

'Well, let's find them!' said Fizza excitedly.

'And how are we going to do that?' asked Billy.

'Operation Scully!' Fizza replied.

After a couple of hours Fizza and the boys had worked out a plan and Fizza typed it onto a piece of paper. It read:

OPERATION SCULLY

TIME: TUESDAY, EIGHT O'CLOCK

1 Scully will be interviewed for 'school magazine' at his house about being a successful factory owner in Birmingham

2 Fletcher and Billy will search Scully's office

3 Fizza will search Scully's email for secrets

The bell rang and Fizza went to answer the door. She discovered Babs, holding a big box of chocolates.

'Oh, hello, Babs,' said Fizza.

The two girls hadn't spoken since Babs had taken Fletcher shopping the day before. Babs held up a piece of paper and began to read.

'Fizza. I have not been nice to you. I was jealous of you and Billy and then I was jealous of you and Fletcher. You seemed to be having such a good time without me, so I tried to get Fletcher to like me instead of you. But I feel bad now—'

'OK, Babs! It's OK!' interrupted Fizza.

However, Babs hadn't finished.

'And I was hurt because Jake had stopped calling me. He's met someone else! Sorry.'

Fizza held her arms out to Babs.

'Oh, Babs, come in!' she said. 'I've got a job for you!'

* * *

At first Babs wasn't sure about going to Scully's

house to interview him.

'But why do *I* have to interview him?' she asked.

'Because we need him out of the way so that we can search his factory,' replied Fletcher.

'But I don't work for the school magazine!' said Babs.

'He won't know that,' said Fletcher.

'But I'm … I'm rubbish at things like that!' said Babs.

'Babs,' said Billy, putting his hand on her arm and smiling at her. His blond hair shone in the Sunday afternoon sunshine and he looked more handsome than ever. 'Of course you can do it – because you're the best.'

Babs looked at him and turned a little red.

'Oh, all right then,' she said.

Chapter 13

Scully is shy of cameras

For two hours on Tuesday evening Fizza sat at her computer in her bedroom. She was trying to get into Scully's computer in his office so that she could read his emails. However, she just couldn't find his secret password. The phone rang. It was Babs.

'Fizza!' Babs whispered. 'I've locked myself in Robert Scully's bathroom! Have you managed to get into his computer yet?'

'Not yet! You'll have to keep Scully busy! How's the interview going?'

'Oh! He really likes himself!' said Babs. 'He has talked for two hours about how rich he is and how many cars he has ... and his wife is yuck! Everything about her is false! Her hair, her nails, probably her teeth! And her skirts are much too short - she's the same age as my mum, for goodness' sake! And she has this silly little dog that she carries everywhere—'

Fizza suddenly interrupted her.

'What's its name?'

'Oh ... Bubble Gum. That's it. That's a stupid name too.'

Fizza typed in the words 'Bubble Gum'. Immediately she got into Robert Scully's emails.

'Babs. You're brilliant!'

'Oh, am I?' said Babs. 'Thanks.'

Fizza started to look through the emails in Robert Scully's computer. She'd never done this before and she was scared. What if she got caught? She'd be in big trouble with Scully. And the police! She knew she had to work quickly.

'OK, Babs! You've got to keep him talking – I don't want him anywhere near his computer while I'm in there!'

'Oh, I wouldn't worry about that – he's on the phone to the police right now.'

Fizza immediately stopped working on her computer.

'The police? Why?'

'Oh, they called him because some robbers have broken into his factory or something.'

'Did they catch them?'

'I don't know – why would I care?' said Babs.

'Because those "robbers" would have been Fletcher and Billy.'

'Oh.'

However, as she finished her call with Babs, Fizza's mobile phone immediately rang again. It was Fletcher.

'Fletcher?' she said. 'Babs said the police rang Scully! Are you OK?'

'Yeah ... but it was close! Billy and I got out just as the police arrived!'

'Did you find anything?' she asked.

'Yeah! Several tins of red paint!' said Fletcher.

As she listened, Fizza worked at her computer searching through Scully's emails.

'And did you manage to get into Scully's emails?' asked Fletcher.

'Yes!' replied Fizza.

'Well? Have you found anything?'

'Oh, yes, Fletcher McIntyre. I think I just have.'

* * *

The next evening Fizza and Fletcher rode Golden and Cloudy out of the centre of Birmingham. Soon the buildings disappeared and it became greener.

'So tell me again what that email said,' said Fletcher.

'It was an email to all his drivers. It said if the other rubbish areas were full, they had to take all the rubbish to the Park Hill area – at night,' replied Fizza.

'So he doesn't want anyone to see him doing that then?'

'No, because he's breaking the law! He isn't getting rid of rubbish in the proper places!'

'And he's getting paid for it. No wonder he's a millionaire!' said Fletcher.

'So now we have to catch him actually doing it!' said Fizza, taking a new mobile phone out of her pocket.

'What? With a phone?'

'Yes, it's my mum's new phone, but it's really good for recording videos!'

'And does your mum know you've got it?'

'No. And she won't because I'll put it back later. I've just borrowed it.'

Eventually they came to a sign above a gate saying: 'Park Hill – the heart of a greener Birmingham.'

The gate led them into a large open green field. There were tall trees all round it. Fizza and Fletcher quickly rode towards the trees to hide. They didn't know how long they'd have to wait. But they hoped that one of Scully's lorries would make an appearance that evening.

*   *   *

It was just getting dark when Fletcher shook Fizza's arm. Fizza opened her eyes; they'd been waiting so long, she must have gone to sleep.

'Look!' he whispered.

Fizza looked in the direction where Fletcher was pointing. In the poor light she could just about see the shape of a large lorry. It was moving very slowly across the large green space.

'They're here!'

There was no mistake about it: it was one of Scully's lorries. As quickly as she could, Fizza took her mum's phone out of her pocket, held it up and pressed the 'record' button. The lorry stopped, its back went up into the air and a huge pile of rubbish was dropped onto the ground.

'Got them!' said Fizza.

Then, suddenly, the phone began to ring.

'Turn it off!' whispered Fletcher. 'They'll hear it!'

Fizza looked at the phone. It said the call was from 'Home.'

'OK!' Fizza replied, but then she decided to answer it in case it was urgent.

'Hello?' she said.

'Fizza? Is that you? What are you doing with my new phone?'

It was her mum!

'Mum! Sorry! I can't talk now! I'll call you later!'

And she hit the 'off' button. Now her mum knew

that she had taken her phone!

'I'm in trouble now,' she thought.

But when she heard the lorry drivers shouting, she realised that they were in even bigger trouble.

'Who's there?'

'It's two kids!'

'Quick!' said Fletcher. 'Let's get back to the horses!'

They ran over to the tree where Golden and Cloudy were waiting for them.

'Follow me!' said Fletcher as he jumped up on Golden and began to ride across the grass. Fizza told herself to be brave and she followed Fletcher as quickly as she could. As they passed the lorry, three big men appeared out of the dark and began to run towards them.

'Come on, girl,' said Fizza to Cloudy. 'We can do it!'

As the men reached out for her, Cloudy suddenly jumped up. Fizza was nearly thrown to the ground, but she just managed to hang on. Then the little horse began to move as fast as her legs would take her across the field and up the road.

'We've lost them!' said Fizza.

'Great!' cried Fletcher.

Eventually, feeling safer, they rode a little more slowly. Fletcher turned and noticed that Fizza had almost stopped.

'Are you OK, Fizza?' he asked.

'Yeah. I'm trying to send a text to Babs,' she said.

This annoyed Fletcher.

'Why do girls always have to send messages to one another – whatever is happening?' he said.

'Because we need a plan!' said Fizza.

Just then they heard the noise of an engine coming up behind them. As she turned to see what it was, Fizza nearly dropped the phone.

'That was close!' she thought. 'Mum would have gone crazy!'

The vehicle came nearer and they saw that it was the rubbish lorry. It was following them!

'Actually, we need a plan right now!' said Fletcher.

He kicked Golden to move more quickly and Fizza, who was beginning to miss her nice warm bed at home, followed him. And they had the ride of their lives through the streets of Birmingham. They went along major roads and down small streets, around roundabouts and under bridges. But the lorry just kept following them. At one point a night bus suddenly appeared; it made Golden jump and Fletcher nearly fell to the ground. Eventually he led them up a path that was too small for the lorry and it couldn't follow any further. At the end of the path Fizza could see the stables! They were safe at last! Quickly they rode into the yard, jumped off the horses and ran into the house.

They found Richard McIntyre sitting at the kitchen table. He looked worried.

'Fletcher! Fizza!' he said. 'Where have you been?'

'It's OK, Richard!' said Fizza. 'We've got a video that shows what Scully has been doing!'

'Yes, and if there's any more trouble from him, we'll take it to the police!' said Fletcher.

At that moment, someone else stepped forward from a dark corner of the room.

'Fletcher! It's good to see you! Your poor father has been worried about you. Well, now that you're here – you can show me that video too, can't you?'

Fizza and Fletcher turned to see Robert Scully standing behind them.

Chapter 14

Big business for the McIntyres

Scully looked at Fletcher and Fizza with his hard eyes.

'I heard you were up on Park Hill,' he said. 'So I thought I'd come and have a cup of tea with your dad while we waited for you.'

'Well, we're back now – so you can go,' said Fletcher.

'No, I can't, young man. Not until I've got your camera.'

'We haven't got a camera,' said Fletcher.

'That's funny,' replied Scully. 'My drivers said you had a camera and that you were filming my lorry!'

Fletcher and Fizza stared at him. It was Richard who spoke next.

'Come on, kids, give the camera to Mr Scully,' he said gently. 'I think it will only make things worse if you don't.'

Fizza took out her mum's mobile phone and put it

on the table.

'It isn't a camera,' she said. 'It's a phone, actually.'

'Nice,' said Scully. 'This phone is very expensive.'

Then as Fizza watched, Scully picked up the phone and dropped it into a mug of tea on the table in front of him.

'Now there's no more video. Actually, there's no more phone!'

Fizza couldn't believe what he'd done. He'd

destroyed her mum's phone. Her mum was going to go crazy!

'That's my mum's! How could you?'

Scully ignored her and stood up to leave.

'Right, I'll say good night then and just so that you don't do anything silly, I think I'll borrow something – to remind you to behave.'

'Like what?' said Richard.

'Well, what about one of your horses? I think I'll take that nice black and white one home.'

'Golden? You can't! We'll call the police!' said Fletcher.

'Well, if you do, it might be the last time you see him.'

And so Richard, Fizza and Fletcher watched as two of Scully's men pulled Golden into the back of a white van. Golden kicked them as hard as he could.

'Go on, boy! Get them!' shouted Fletcher.

As Golden was finally driven away in the back of the van, another of Scully's drivers parked a lorry in front of the stable gate. It meant that Richard's carriages couldn't leave the stables.

'Just in case you get any silly ideas!' said Scully, laughing. He got into his car and drove off into the night.

As they watched Scully disappear, the three of them felt completely helpless.

'I'm going to follow him!' said Fletcher.

'Hold on!' said his father. 'Let's not do anything that might put Golden in danger!'

Fletcher fell into an angry silence. Then Fizza suddenly remembered something.

'Oh! How could I be so stupid!' she exclaimed.

Fletcher and Richard looked at her in surprise.

'Richard, have you checked your emails tonight?' she asked.

'No. I've been a little busy!' he replied.

'Well, you've got time to look now!'

* * *

A few moments later Richard came back, smiling.

'Fizza McIntyre, you are one clever girl,' he laughed.

'What has she done?' asked Fletcher.

'She emailed me the video of Scully's lorry on Park Hill from her mum's phone!'

It meant they still had the video that could be used against Scully!

'Now what do we do?' asked Fletcher, but before anyone could reply they were interrupted by a taxi stopping outside. Billy and Babs got out.

'I got your text!' said Babs.

'What's happened?' asked Billy.

Fizza and Fletcher explained as quickly as they could.

'Poor Golden!' said Babs.

'Well, I think the police would love to see a copy of that video, don't you?' said Richard.

'You do that, Dad, but I'm going to get Golden back from Scully's house!' said Fletcher.

'I know where he lives!' said Babs.

'OK!' said Billy. 'Let's go!'

'We can't! We can't get the carriages out because of the lorry!' said Fizza.

'Oh, don't worry about that,' said Billy, climbing up and looking into the rubbish lorry. Everyone stared at him.

'Did I mention that my dad is a lorry driver?' he shouted. 'He often leaves the keys in his lorry – and *they've* left them too!'

He started the engine.

'But that's stealing!' said Babs.

'I'm not stealing it!' he laughed. 'I'm just moving it. And then we can get the carriages out.'

* * *

'This is the best!' said Billy, as Fletcher drove the horse and carriage through the quiet streets of Birmingham.

'Yeah!' said Babs. 'All taxis should be like this!'

Fizza smiled to herself. Billy and Babs were behaving like two excited children going for a pony ride.

Eventually, Fletcher turned the carriage into a quiet road with large, expensive houses on each side. They looked at all the houses until they saw one with a large gold 'S' on the iron gate.

'That's Scully's house!' said Babs. 'I recognise his cars!'

Sure enough, there were several expensive cars parked on the drive. Billy whistled.

'Nice,' he said.

Fletcher stopped the carriage across the street, where they were hidden by a large tree.

'Look!' he said.

The gates to Scully's house were open and they could see a white van. It was the van that had taken Golden away.

'Come on, Fletcher!' whispered Fizza. 'Let's get your horse back!'

She jumped down from the carriage and ran across the road. Fletcher followed her. They saw two men climb down from the van and disappear round the back of Scully's house. The gates were still open, so Fizza and Fletcher ran quietly into the driveway and went to where the van was.

'Golden!' whispered Fletcher. 'Are you in there?'

They heard a loud kick from inside the van.

'He's in there,' smiled Fizza.

Fletcher started to pull on the back door.

'It's OK, boy, I'll get you out,' he said.

At that moment the gates began to close. They were going to be locked inside! Then they heard an ugly little laugh.

'Have you lost something, kids?'

Fizza and Fletcher turned round to see Robert Scully standing at his front door.

'Now, let me see,' he said. 'One: you're on my land. Two: you're stealing my van. I think you're breaking the law, don't you? Shall we see what the police think? I'll give them a call, shall I?'

He pulled his mobile phone from his top pocket. At this moment, they heard another laugh. This time it was Billy. He had his face pressed against the gate.

'I wouldn't worry about that, Mr Scully!' he

shouted. 'They're already here!'

Fizza, Fletcher and Scully listened. They heard the unmistakable sound of a police car. As soon as it stopped, the back door opened and Richard McIntyre got out. He was holding a CD of the video of Scully's lorry dropping rubbish on Park Hill.

What a night it had been! And the next few days were even more extraordinary. Robert Scully lost his business because, with the help of the video, the police discovered that he was responsible for all of the rubbish left in green areas in Birmingham. Fizza and Fletcher (and Billy and Babs) were in all the newspapers. There were photos of the Bullring Kid and the Country Cowboy everywhere.

The Richard McIntyre Horse and Carriage Company became a huge success. People wanted to use the carriages for all sorts of reasons, which included getting to work, going out to dinner and getting married! The number of passengers grew and extra horses and carriages were brought in to help. Birmingham was very, very proud of its new, 'green' taxi service.

* * *

Then one day Richard McIntyre invited Fizza and her parents to his house for Sunday lunch. He cooked a special meal. He had borrowed the recipe from Fizza's mum.

'That was delicious, Richard!' said Rubel.

'Mmm!' said Imran.

'And what did *you* think of *my* fish curry, Fizza?' asked Richard.

'It was nicer than ... Robert Scully!' she said.

And they all laughed because everything was nicer than Robert Scully. Then Richard was suddenly serious.

'Listen, kids. I have some news for you.'

He paused. Fletcher and Fizza looked at him. They both knew something was wrong.

'I have decided to return to Sark,' he said.

'But why, Dad?' said Fletcher.

'Birmingham's not for me, son.'

'But you can't!' said Fizza. 'The business is such a success!'

'Well, here's another surprise!' said her dad. 'Richard has asked us if we would like to run his business in Birmingham.'

'While he goes back to take care of the one on Sark!' added her mum.

'So there will be a Birmingham McIntyre Horse

and Carriage Company ...' laughed Imran.

'And a Sark one!' said Richard.

'And if the business does well, we're even hoping to buy Scully's land!' said her mum.

Fizza couldn't believe what she was hearing. This was exciting news and terrible news all at the same time!

'And listen to this, Fletcher,' said Richard. 'You don't have to go. You can stay with Rubel, Imran and Fizza.'

Fletcher paused. He looked at Fizza and then at his dad.

'It's OK, Dad,' he said quietly. 'I'll come home with you.'

He smiled at Fizza. She smiled back, but she couldn't stop the tears running down her face.

* * *

And so, once again Fizza stood beside Richard McIntyre as he arranged the suitcases. This time he wasn't loading them onto a boat, he was loading them onto a horse lorry; and it wasn't her luggage, it was Fletcher's. As she helped them put their bags in, she remembered what she'd been like at the beginning of the summer holidays – shy, quiet, perhaps even a little dull? Fletcher McIntyre had changed her! He'd made her who she was now! OK, Billy and Babs were good friends, but Fletcher was so much more than that.

She was too shy to tell him, but she didn't want him to go.

'Fizza?'

She turned to see Fletcher standing behind her.

'Well, we're ready to go,' he said.

'Great!' she lied, smiling.

Fletcher looked at her. He wasn't going to miss Birmingham but, the truth was, he did not want to leave Fizza. This girl had changed him. She had stopped him being angry, bad-tempered and rude. She had taught him how to have fun and how to make friends!

But now she looked happy! Perhaps she didn't care that he was going! After all, he thought, she's got Billy!

They stood facing one another without speaking. She could see a boy who had wide green eyes and little brown freckles on his nose, and he could see a girl with warm, kind eyes and thick black hair that curled round her pretty face. They spoke at exactly the same moment.

'I don't want to go, you know,' he said.

'I don't want you to go, you know,' she said.

And then they laughed.

'But I've got to go with Dad – he hasn't got anyone else.'

'I understand. I'd do the same.'

'And try not to get into any more trouble – at least not without me, that is.'

'What do you mean?'

'Well, if there's any trouble in Birmingham, I should be there.'

Fizza smiled. Suddenly she felt a lot happier. 'And if there's any trouble in Sark, I should be there!' she said.

'See you around, Bullring Kid.'

'See you, Country Cowboy.'

Fletcher McIntyre climbed into the horse lorry beside his dad and, within seconds, they had completely disappeared from view.

Learning guide | 学习指导

Chapter 1

New words 生词

- chance /tʃɑːns/ *n.*（尤指希望发生的事的）可能性，巧合
- complain /kəmˈpleɪn/ *v.* 抱怨
- council /ˈkaʊnsl/ *n.*（市、郡等的）政务委员会，地方议会
- curry /ˈkʌri/ *n.* 咖喱
- eventually /ɪˈventʃuəli/ *ad.* 最终
- falsely /ˈfɔːlsli/ *ad.* 虚假地，虚伪地
- greedily /ˈgriːdɪli/ *ad.* 贪吃地，贪婪地
- horrible /ˈhɒrəbl/ *a.* 令人恐惧的
- interrupt /ˌɪntəˈrʌpt/ *v.* 打断，插话
- makeup /ˈmeɪkʌp/ *n.* 化妆品
- mouthful /ˈmaʊθfʊl/ *n.*（食物或饮料的）一口，一满口
- pollution /pəˈluːʃn/ *n.* 污染
- spoonful /ˈspuːnfʊl/ *n.* 一勺的量
- trainer /ˈtreɪnə(r)/ *n.* 运动鞋

Phrases & expressions 短语和表达

- by surprise 出其不意地
- go out with ... 和……交往
- information technology 信息技术
- leave sb. alone 不打扰某人，不接触某人
- make progress 取得进步

- on fire 着火
- pick oneself. up（跌倒或被击倒后）慢慢站起身
- school uniform 校服
- sweet talk 甜言蜜语
- take up sth. 开始从事某事

Cultural notes 文化点滴

• Birmingham: 伯明翰，仅次于伦敦的英国第二大国际化城市，地处英格兰中部，交通四通八达，拥有跨国公司、研发中心、世界知名大学及创新企业，是一个繁荣的商业城市。

• curry: 咖喱，由多种香料调配而成的酱料，常见于印度菜、泰国菜和日本菜等亚洲地区菜系，一般伴随肉类和饭一起吃。

• Sark: 萨克岛，位于英吉利海峡中海峡群岛的一个岛。萨克岛上禁止使用汽车，可使用的交通工具只有马车、脚踏车，以及老人及行动不便者可使用的以电池驱动的四轮休闲车或电动脚踏车。萨克岛的主要产业是观光业及金融业。

• the Channel Islands: 海峡群岛，位于英吉利海峡，由泽西岛（Jersey）、根西岛（Guernsey）、奥尔德尼岛（Alderney）和萨克岛（Sark）等岛屿组成。群岛风景优美，花卉繁多，草木茂盛，具有温暖宜人的海洋性气候，为游览胜地。

Chapter 2

New words 生词

- admit /əd'mɪt/ *v.* 承认

- arrival /əˈraɪvl/ *n.* 到来
- breath /breθ/ *n.* 呼吸
- dull /dʌl/ *a.* 木讷的，无趣的
- explode /ɪkˈspləʊd/ *v.* 爆炸
- haircut /ˈheəkʌt/ *n.* 发型；理发
- hairy /ˈheəri/ *a.* 多毛的
- obviously /ˈɒbviəsli/ *ad.* 显然
- pollution-free /pəˌluːʃn ˈfriː/ *a.* 没有污染的
- proper /ˈprɒpə(r)/ *a.* 正式的
- recognise /ˈrekəgnaɪz/ *v.* 认出
- whisper /ˈwɪspə(r)/ *v.* 耳语，低语

Phrases & expressions 短语和表达

- hairdresser /ˈheədresə(r)/ *n.* 理发师
- in embarrassment 窘迫地，尴尬地
- walk straight into ... 迎面撞上……

Cultural note 文化点滴

- the Bullring Shopping Centre in Birmingham: 伯明翰斗牛场购物中心，英国伯明翰市中心的一座现代购物中心，是英国最大的购物中心之一，每年吸引着大量的游客光顾。购物中心的一个门口有一尊著名的牛雕塑。

Reading exercises 阅读练习

1. Check your answers to Before reading on page 4.

2. Complete the summary of Chapters 1 and 2 with the words in the box.

Felicity	Greece	Babs (x2)	Sark	Billy
Rubel	Imran	judo	Birmingham	

Fizza, whose real name is ________ , lives with her parents in a big, busy city in the middle of England called ________. Her mum, ________ , works for the local council. Her dad, ________ , loves two things in life – fish curry, which Fizza hates, and his favourite sport, ________ , which he teaches Fizza in the garden. Fizza, however, prefers spending time working on her computer. It's her best subject at school, but her mum thinks she spends too much time on it. Fizza's best friend, ________ , is very different. She's more interested in fashion and boys, especially ________ Adams, who goes to the same school. On the last day of school, everyone is talking about the exciting places they are going to in the summer. ________ , for example, is going sailing in ________. Fizza, however, is too embarrassed to tell everyone that she is only going to ________ , a quiet island with no cars.

3. Are the sentences true (T) or false (F)?
   a) Fizza is looking forward to her holiday.
   b) Fizza's dad doesn't think she's good at judo.
   c) Babs and Fizza don't wear the same kind of clothes.
   d) The other girls at school look older than Fizza.
   e) Fizza was working when Billy came into the classroom.
   f) Fizza had her hair cut for Billy.
   g) Billy was interested in Fizza when he saw her at the shopping centre.

4. Match the two parts of the sentences.

____1) Fizza doesn't want to join a judo club because

____2) Fizza wants to be cool although

____3) Babs is very embarrassed when

____4) Fizza is surprised when

a) she doesn't admit it to anyone.

b) Billy speaks to her and the other girls.

c) Billy says she is cool.

d) it's not cool.

5. Answer the questions.

a) Why is Sark a good place for Rubel to go on holiday?

b) Why are the other girls surprised that Billy spoke to Fizza?

6. Tick (√) what you think happens in the next four chapters.

a) Billy becomes Fizza's boyfriend. ☐

b) Billy becomes Babs's boyfriend. ☐

c) Fizza has a good time on holiday. ☐

Chapter 3

New words 生词

- carriage /ˈkærɪdʒ/ *n.* 马车
- completely /kəmˈpliːtli/ *ad.* 完全地
- cottage /ˈkɒtɪdʒ/ *n.* 乡村小屋，村舍
- cross /krɒs/ *a.* 生气的
- curly /ˈkɜːli/ *a.* 卷曲的
- defeat /dɪˈfiːt/ *n.* 失败
- discover /dɪˈskʌvə(r)/ *v.* 发现
- exactly /ɪɡˈzæktli/ *ad.* 恰好地
- explore /ɪkˈsplɔː(r)/ *v.* 探索

- harbour /ˈhɑːbə(r)/ *n.* 港口
- jug /dʒʌg/ *n.* 水壶
- move /muːv/ *n.* 招式
- queue /kjuː/ *n.* 队列 *v.* 排队等候
- rocky /ˈrɒki/ *a.* 多岩石的
- suitcase /ˈsuːtkeɪs/ *n.* 行李箱
- suntanned /ˈsʌntænd/ *a.* 被太阳晒黑的，晒成古铜色的
- yawn /jɔːn/ *v.* 打哈欠

Phrases & expressions 短语和表达

- breathe in 吸气
- come to a stop 停止
- in a bad mood 心情不好
- in the distance 在远处

Chapter 4

New words 生词

- ankle /ˈæŋkl/ *n.* 脚踝
- annoy /əˈnɔɪ/ *v.* 惹恼
- crash /kræʃ/ *v.*（发出巨响的）猛撞，坠落
- guilty /ˈgɪlti/ *a.* 愧疚的
- mystery /ˈmɪstri/ *n.* 神秘
- pile /paɪl/ *n.* 堆
- rudely /ˈruːdli/ *ad.* 粗鲁地

Phrases & expressions 短语和表达

- apart from ... 除了……
- change the subject 换话题
- fishing rod 钓竿
- get rid of ... 摆脱……
- spy on ... 暗中监视……
- turn one's back on ... 不理睬……

Chapter 5

New words 生词

- escape /ɪˈskeɪp/ *v.* 逃脱
- freckle /ˈfrekl/ *n.* 雀斑
- mug /mʌg/ *n.* 圆筒形有柄大杯
- position /pəˈzɪʃn/ *n.* 位置
- rub /rʌb/ *v.* 擦
- scream /skriːm/ *v.* 尖叫
- square /skweə(r)/ *a.* 方形的
- stable /ˈsteɪbl/ *n.* 马厩
- stroke /strəʊk/ *v.* 抚摸，轻抚
- whistle /ˈwɪsl/ *v.* 吹口哨

Phrases & expressions 短语和表达

- just in time 正及时
- pull sb. onto one's feet 把某人拉起来
- side by side 并排
- stay behind 留下来

Chapter 6

New words 生词

- bat /bæt/ *n.* 蝙蝠
- bottom /ˈbɒtəm/ *n.* 屁股
- date /deɪt/ *n.* 约会；约定
- patiently /ˈpeɪʃntli/ *ad.* 耐心地
- processor /ˈprəʊsesə(r)/ *n.* 处理器
- saddle /ˈsædl/ *n.* 马鞍
- stuff /stʌf/ *n.* 东西
- trick /trɪk/ *n.* 技巧，窍门，把戏
- untie /ʌnˈtaɪ/ *v.* 解开

Phrases & expressions 短语和表达

- bad egg 坏家伙
- chase after ... 追赶……
- fall in love with ... 爱上……
- get caught in ... 卡在……里
- leather strap（马具上的）皮带
- light year 光年
- take off 起飞，离开

Reading exercises 阅读练习

1. Complete the sentences with the names in the box.

Rubel	Fizza (x2)	Fletcher (x3)	Richard (x2)

a) ____________ thinks that Sark is exciting.

b) ____________ changes her opinion of Sark.

c) ______________ shows Fizza and her parents the island.

d) ______________ falls out of a tree.

e) ______________ has a judo lesson.

f) ______________ shows Fizza the island's secrets.

g) ______________ is the Bullring Kid.

h) ______________ is the Country Cowboy.

2. Underline the correct word in each sentence.

a) Fizza doesn't buy a newspaper because they *aren't sold / hadn't arrived* on Sark.

b) On the first night of the holiday, Fizza sees someone watching her from *a tree / a horse*.

c) Fizza doesn't go to the restaurant with her parents because she *is tired / has a reason for staying at home.*

d) Fizza *wants / doesn't want* to visit the pot-maker.

e) Before going to Sark, Fizza *was afraid of / didn't like* horses.

f) Her first horse riding lesson helps Fizza stop thinking about *Sark /Birmingham*.

g) Fletcher gets *ice cream / a bat* out of Fizza's hair.

3. What do the underlined words refer to in these lines from the text?

a) 'Isn't this exciting, Fizza!' (page 20) __________________________

b) 'It's a beautiful little beach ...' (page 28) ______________

c) It was a tall boy wearing jeans ... (page 32) ___________________

d) She didn't want to see that rude boy! (page 36) ________

e) 'Yeah, but don't tell him, he doesn't know that!' (page 40) ____ ____________

f) 'I mean, that will be great!' (page 46) ______________

g) 'How do you do that?' (page 48) ______________

4. Answer the questions.
   a) Why is Sark 'the island that time forgot'?
   b) How does Fizza feel when she says 'It's a date!'? (page 45)
   c) Why does Fletcher prefer animals to people?
   d) What happens at the end of Chapter 6?

Chapter 7

New words 生词

- coat /kəʊt/ *n.*（动物）皮毛
- divorce /dɪˈvɔːs/ *v.* 离婚
- kidnapper /ˈkɪdnæpə(r)/ *n.* 绑架者
- moonlit /ˈmuːnlɪt/ *a.* 月光照耀下的
- saucepan /ˈsɔːspən/ *n.* 炖锅，深平底锅
- sharply /ˈʃɑːpli/ *ad.* 尖刻地，锐利地
- steal /stiːl/ *v.* 偷
- trap /træp/ *n.* 陷阱，圈套
- unmistakable /ˌʌnmɪˈsteɪkəbl/ *a.* 不会弄错的，确定无疑的

Phrases & expressions 短语和表达

- at present 目前
- be fed up with ... 受够了……
- be supposed to do sth. 应该做某事
- hold one's breath 屏住呼吸
- more than ... 比……还多
- take hold of ... 抓住……
- under one's breath 不敢出气

Chapter 8

New words 生词

- engine /ˈendʒɪn/ *n.* 马达
- familiar /fəˈmɪliə(r)/ *a.* 熟悉的
- flash /flæʃ/ *v.* 闪光
- ignore /ɪɡˈnɔː(r)/ *v.* 忽视，对……不予理会
- loudspeaker /ˌlaʊdˈspiːkə(r)/ *n.* 扩音器
- miserable /ˈmɪzrəbl/ *a.* 痛苦的，非常难受的
- unload /ˌʌnˈləʊd/ *v.* 从（车、船等）卸下（货物）

Phrases & expressions 短语和表达

- after all 终究
- be flooded with ... 被……所淹没
- knock sb. down 击倒某人
- lay a trap 设下陷阱，设下圈套
- pull sth. free from ... 把某物从……抽出
- under control 得到控制

Chapter 9

New words 生词

- adventure /ədˈventʃə(r)/ *n.* 历险（经历），奇遇
- apology /əˈpɒlədʒi/ *n.* 道歉
- behaviour /bɪˈheɪvjə(r)/ *n.* 行为
- corridor /ˈkɒrɪdɔː(r)/ *n.* 走廊

- romance /rəʊˈmæns/ *n.* 恋爱，爱情
- suntan /ˈsʌntæn/ *n.* 晒黑
- text /tekst/ *n.* 短信，短消息

Phrases & expressions 短语和表达

- be responsible for ... 对……负责
- get into trouble 陷入麻烦
- take the blame 承担过错
- tell sb. off 训斥某人
- walk sb. home 陪某人走回家

Chapter 10

New words 生词

- ambulance /ˈæmbjələns/ *n.* 救护车
- apparently /əˈpærəntli/ *ad.* 据说
- arrange /əˈreɪndʒ/ *v.* 安排
- astonishment /əˈstɒnɪʃmənt/ *n.* 惊讶
- bad-tempered /ˌbæd ˈtempəd/ *a.* 脾气不好的
- fortnight /ˈfɔːtnaɪt/ *n.* 两个星期
- previous /ˈpriːviəs/ *a.* 之前的
- unlikeable /ʌnˈlaɪkəbl/ *a.* 不讨人喜欢的

Phrases & expressions 短语和表达

- be jealous of ... 嫉妒……
- be shy of ... 害怕……，羞于……
- carry on doing sth. 继续做某事
- in return 作为回报，作为交换

Reading exercises 阅读练习

1. Are the sentences true (T) or false (F)?
   a) Only one policeman works on Sark.
   b) Fletcher hasn't seen his mum for ten years.
   c) The men are going to kill the horses.
   d) Richard called the police in Guernsey and told them to come to Sark.
   e) The headmaster is surprised that it was Fizza who changed the photos.
   f) Rubel shares lots of secret information from her work with Fizza.
   g) A new student arrives in Fizza's class.
   h) Fizza forgets an arrangement she made.
2. Underline the correct words in each sentence.
   a) Horses have been stolen from *two / three* islands.
   b) Fizza and Fletcher use Cloudy because she's a *light colour / good horse*.
   c) *Fizza / Fletcher* stops the fat man who's trying to steal Cloudy.
   d) At the end of the holiday, Fizza *wants / doesn't want* to leave Sark.
   e) Fizza and Billy have to *talk / write* to their teachers to say sorry.
   f) Fizza takes a walk in the park with *Babs / Billy*.
   g) Fletcher finds being at his new school *difficult / easy*.
   h) *A teacher / Fizza* stops the fight between Billy and Fletcher.
3. What do the underlined words refer to in these sentences from the text?
   a) 'I've never spoken to anyone about it before,' (page 54)
   b) 'That's the sign! They're here!' (page 59)

c) And this had made them local heroes. (page 63)
d) 'It was cool.' (page 65)
e) 'Sir, it was my idea,' (page 68)
f) 'That would be nice,' (page 73)
g) 'We were really lucky to get it,' (page 76)
h) ... she wasn't sure if she liked it. (page 82)

5. Answer the questions.
a) Why did Fletcher's mum leave?
b) How does Fizza think that Fletcher feels about her leaving Sark?
c) What do Fizza's friends think of Fletcher?
d) Why do you think Fletcher and Billy fight?

5. Tick (√) what you think happens in the final chapters.
a) Fizza chooses Billy to be her boyfriend. □
b) Fletcher goes back to Sark to live. □
c) Fizza goes to Sark to live. □

Chapter 11

New words 生词

- corner /ˈkɔːnə(r)/ *v.* 使走投无路
- equally /ˈiːkwəli/ *ad.* 同样地
- growl /graʊl/ *v.* 嚎叫

Phrases & expressions 短语和表达

- bend down 弯下腰
- hold onto ... 紧紧抓住……

- in an attempt to do sth. 试图做某事

Chapter 12

New words 生词

- eyelash /ˈaɪlæʃ/ *n.* 眼睫毛
- interview /ˈɪntəvjuː/ *v.* 采访
- laughter /ˈlɑːftə(r)/ *n.* 笑声
- mean /miːn/ *a.* 刻薄的，小气的
- operation /ˌɒpəˈreɪʃn/ *n.* 行动
- upset /ʌpˈset/ *a.* 难过的，沮丧的

Phrases & expressions 短语和表达

- hold one's arms out to ... 向……伸出双臂
- kind of ... 有点儿……
- pull away 离开
- used to be 曾经是
- work out 找到（解决办法等）

Chapter 13

New words 生词

- millionaire /ˌmɪljəˈneə(r)/ *n.* 百万富翁
- password /ˈpɑːswɜːd/ *n.* 密码
- robber /ˈrɒbə(r)/ *n.* 盗贼
- roundabout /ˈraʊndəbaʊt/ *n.* 环状交叉路口，交通环岛

- urgent /ˈɜːdʒənt/ *a.* 紧急的
- vehicle /ˈviːəkl/ *n.* 交通工具，车辆
- yuck /jʌk/ *a.* 令人恶心的

Phrases & expressions 短语和表达

- hang on 坚持住
- in case 以防
- look through ... 浏览……
- make an appearance 出现
- no wonder ... 怪不得……
- now that ... 既然……
- What if ...? 如果……怎么办？

Chapter 14

New words 生词

- behave /bɪˈheɪv/ *v.* 举止端正
- copy /ˈkɒpi/ *n.* 副本
- driveway /ˈdraɪvweɪ/ *n.* 私人车道
- exclaim /ɪkˈskleɪm/ *v.* 惊叫，呼喊
- extraordinary /ɪkˈstrɔːdnri/ *a.* 非凡的
- load /ləʊd/ *v.* 装载
- remind /rɪˈmaɪnd/ *v.* 提醒
- van /væn/ *n.*（厢式）小型货车

Phrases & expressions 短语和表达

- all sorts of ... 各种各样的……
- drive off 开走

- hard eyes 冷酷的眼神
- press sth. against ... 把某物紧贴在……

Reading exercises 阅读练习

1. Complete the sentences with the names in the box.

Billy   Scully (x3)   Babs (x2)   Fizza   Fletcher

a) ____________ wants the land where the stables are.
b) ____________ is frightened by a dog.
c) ____________ is taken shopping by some new friends.
d) ____________ apologises for not being nice.
e) ____________ interviews someone.
f) ____________ has the name of a dog as a password.
g) ____________ destroys a mobile phone.
h) ____________ sends an email from a mobile phone.

2. Put the sentences in order.

a) Fizza discovers Scully's password. □
b) Fletcher phones Fizza. □
c) Babs phones Fizza. □
d) Fletcher and Billy manage to escape from the factory. □
e) The police go to Scully's factory. □
f) Babs goes to interview Scully. □
g) Fizza gets into Scully's email account. □
h) Fizza finds an interesting email. □

3. Match the two parts of the sentences.

____________ 1) Scully's drivers make lots of noise with their lorries
____________ 2) Billy's father lost his job with Scully before
____________ 3) When Fizza reads Scully's emails, she discovers that

____________ 4) When Fizza and Fletcher go to Park Hill, they see

____________ 5) Scully puts Fizza's mum's phone in the mug of tea because

____________ 6) Scully says Golden may disappear if

____________ 7) They manage to get the horse and carriage out because

____________ 8) Scully loses his business after the police see

a) anyone calls the police.

b) he could find out any secrets.

c) Billy moves the lorry.

d) he had told his drivers to get rid of rubbish in Park Hill.

e) he wants to destroy Fizza's video.

f) Scully's men getting rid of rubbish there.

g) the video Fizza made.

h) to frighten the horses.

4. Answer the questions.

a) How does Fletcher help Billy with the black dog?

b) How does Fizza feel about Fletcher becoming more popular?

c) What does Babs think of Scully's wife?

d) How do Fizza and Fletcher get back to the stable from Park Hill?

e) What's going to happen to Richard's green taxi service in Birmingham?

f) How does Fizza feel about Fletcher leaving Birmingham?

Translation
参考译文

斗牛场酷妞与乡村牛仔

第 1 章　柔道小孩儿

第5页

“哎哟！”

菲扎的爸爸第五次把她过肩摔到草地上。

“啊！我没准备好，爸爸！”她喊道。

“那不是理由，菲扎！你必须时刻准备着！”她爸爸回答，“虽然你是个女孩儿，但那并不妨碍你和男人一样勇敢。”

菲扎从地上费力起身，面向她的柔道老师。依姆兰 · 麦金太尔有一半苏格兰、一半巴基斯坦血统，却是个百分之百不知退缩的人。他们在傍晚的阳光里练习柔道已经一个多小时了，她现在真的很累。不过，她还是出其不意地成功拿下她老爸。尽管她感到支撑不住了，但她还是猛地冲过去，将他摔倒在地。

“菲扎！饶了你可怜的老爸吧！”妈妈在屋里喊道，“不管怎样，到下午茶时间了。”

“多谢了，鲁贝尔！你从这个疯狂的柔道小孩儿手里救了我！”依姆兰说。

他站起来，拉过菲扎的手，他们一起笑着走进了房子。

第7页

今天是周四，所以菲扎知道妈妈做了什么茶点。每周都是一样的，因为那是她爸爸最喜欢的食物。

“哦，不要啊，我讨厌咖喱鱼！”菲扎坐到桌边时想。

咖喱鱼总是那么辣，让她嘴巴像着火一样，而且她讨厌鱼。但是，为了让爸爸妈妈开心，她没有抱怨就吃了起来。

“那么，你盼着我们的假期吗，菲扎？”她爸爸问。

“不——”菲扎想。

“肯定啊，她盼着呢！”妈妈插了一句，“不是吗，宝贝？”

菲扎含着满口难吃的咖喱挤出笑脸。

“我等不及了！我爱海峡群岛，但这还是我第一次去萨克岛。”菲扎的爸爸边说边又贪馋地从碗里舀了一大勺食物，“它是群岛里最小的岛，是吧？”

“对，那儿不让开汽车，所以会很安静！空气清新，还没有污染！”妈妈说。

“多美妙啊！”依姆兰说。

第8页

“多没劲啊！”菲扎想。

菲扎的妈妈鲁贝尔在伯明翰地方议会的环境办公室工作。她的工作职责是让伯明翰更清洁、更“绿色”，但这是一份很难做的工作，因为这座城市里有那么多汽车和工厂，而且垃圾也太多。所以在一个没有汽车的岛上度假是她理想中的完美假日。但是，那不是菲扎理想中的完美假日。她热爱城市，她热爱伯明翰！这里热闹！这里喧哗！这里才是家！

“好了！”依姆兰吃完东西后说，“来吧，菲扎——我们再练会儿柔道。”

“可我想去玩电脑。”菲扎说。

“费莉西蒂，”妈妈说，“你总玩电脑。”

这说的是实情，菲扎喜欢电脑。她花了好多时间来琢磨不同的程序，而且她是班里信息技术课学得最好的学生。她知道自己擅长的就是这门课程。

“可我想和朋友聊天。”她回答。

“你不能用手机吗？”妈妈说，“还有更好的做法，去找他们啊——像我小时候那样。”

“若不练习柔道，你就不会再有进步的！”她爸爸说。

第9页

菲扎深深地叹了口气。总是这样，妈妈觉得她用电脑太多，爸爸觉得她应该成为奥运会柔道冠军。

菲扎的爸爸认为柔道是世界上最重要的事情。他不是在练柔道，就是在谈柔道。他从小就开始学习柔道，最终成为苏格兰的冠军。然而，菲扎并不像她爸爸那样热爱柔道。

“说实话，菲扎，我觉得你真的一直在进步。”他说，“你还会成为冠军！但是我告诉过你，你该加入个柔道俱乐部！”

菲扎再一次叹了口气。在花园练练柔道不算什么，但她不愿意加入俱乐部，因为柔道并不“酷”。她最好的朋友芭布丝不练柔道，其他“酷”女孩儿也都不练柔道。

“爸爸！您犯傻呀？”她说。

“你说什么？”她爸爸说。

“您什么都教给我了，俱乐部还能教我什么呢？”菲扎说。

甜言蜜语逗得依姆兰大笑起来，菲扎则从桌旁迅速站起身来。

第10页

“来吧，老头儿。我们比赛跑到花园，我保证对您手下留情！”

* * *

大约六点半，门铃响了。

“菲扎！”妈妈冲楼上喊，“芭布丝来啦！”

菲扎跑下楼，她朋友正在门厅等着她。

“嗨，芭布丝！”她说。

“菲扎！我得来跟你说个事！”芭布丝说，她显然很兴奋。

“哦？什么事？”

“我刚去了商店，你猜我在公交车上看到了谁？”她说。

“女王？”

“什么？不是，别傻啦。比利·亚当斯！”

“谁？”

“菲扎！你知道的！就是我们学校特别帅的那个男生！”

芭布丝想约比利出去玩儿，但他们年级所有的女孩儿也都这么想。他很受女孩儿青睐。

“然后呢？”菲扎说。

“然后什么？”芭布丝回应。

第11页

“然后，发生什么了？”

“嗯，他看了看我。嗯，我觉得他看了我——他看向我附近，因为他坐在我前面。”

“看来他在整个车厢里选中你了？”

“对啊！”

菲扎不想说比利坐在她前面可能只是巧合。

“哇！”她回答道。

“我知道！”芭布丝说。

菲扎微笑着。自从她11岁那年来到这个学校以后，她和芭布丝就是好朋友了。四年了，她们做什么事都形影不离：一起欢笑，一起玩幼稚的游戏，一起说悄悄话，然后再接着哈哈大笑。但是，最近菲扎觉得有什么地方变了，因为芭布丝的生活中有新的东西闯入。实际上，有两样新东西：男孩子和潮流。芭布丝开始不再穿校服，而且她开始和那些令人侧目的“酷”女孩儿一样着装。而尽管菲扎暗自也想变“酷”，但是她仍然穿着校服，在校外她也不过是穿牛仔裤、T恤衫和运动鞋。她真的对穿奇装异服或者化妆不感兴趣，尤其是为了男孩子而那样打扮。

第12页

菲扎的妈妈说她好看，但是，她想自己妈妈当然会那么说，不是吗？她长着一头浓密的黑发，却总是扎在后面。她还有一双棕色的眼睛、一只塌鼻子和一张她觉得让她看起来像青蛙的嘴。她瘦小的身材也没带来什么好处，因为这身材使得她比所有别的15岁女孩儿看起来年纪都要小。

菲扎知道她和芭布丝仍然可以做朋友，她们还可以继续说悄悄话。但现在悄悄话的内容已经不一样了，它们不再是关于那些可爱的动物宝宝或者是街的尽头一栋闹鬼的房子，它们会和比利那样的男孩子有关了。

“哦，”菲扎说，“他明天会上学的！”

“哎呀！我知道！我知道！”芭布丝说，“我等不及了！我要去跟他搭话！菲扎，你要帮我啊！”

第 2 章　菲扎“酷”了十分钟

第13页

第二天是学期的最后一天，没有什么正式的课。那一天大家都不想学习。好几百个学生从一个教室走到另一个教室，热烈地谈论着暑假。菲扎坐在计算机房听着别人聊天。她听到有人说去迪士尼乐园，有人说去美国参加夏令营，还有人去西班牙、意大利或葡萄牙度假。芭布丝正在跟班里一群“酷”得要命的女孩儿们谈论假期和表亲们去希腊航海旅行的事。菲扎假装在电脑前忙着，那样就不用告诉任何人她那个要去非常安静、没有污染的萨克岛的假期了。

突然，四个男孩儿边笑边嚷地跑进教室。菲扎注意到其中一位是比利·亚当斯，就是芭布丝前一天晚上在公交车上看到的那个“特别帅的男生”。当菲扎看到芭布丝难为情地用手捂着脸的时候，她暗自笑了起来。男孩儿们的到来使得那帮“酷”女孩儿们兴奋地窃窃私语。这些男孩儿不在乎学习，只想要找乐子。他们总是受到老师们的训斥，这却使得他们在女生面前更显魅力。菲扎不自在地躲在电脑后。

第14页

“这里谁电脑用得好？”比利问。

女孩儿们互相看着。她们都知道如何用聊天室，但别的就不怎么会了。

“怎么了？”有个女孩儿问。

“我需要找人帮我处理一些照片。”

“我知道谁能帮你，比利！”有人用有点儿过分响亮的声音说。

菲扎从电脑后伸头去看是谁说的，她惊讶地发现说话的是满脸通红的芭布丝。比利·亚当斯转过脸去看着她，她的脸从红色变成了紫色！菲扎觉得她那可怜的朋友窘得都快爆炸了。

“哦？”他说。

“菲扎。”

“谁？”比利说。

芭布丝指了指菲扎。

“那是菲扎，她电脑技术超棒。”

第15页

大伙儿都看向菲扎。她想要躲到桌子下面去。

“噢，太好了。谢谢。”比利说完就走到菲扎的座位旁。

“嗨，菲扎。”他说。

“嗨。”她好不容易轻轻地回了一声。

“你可以弄一下这个吗？”他说着在她边上坐下来，递过一张光盘。她眼睛盯着光盘。

“这是老师们的照片，”他微笑着说，“我想送给他们一份期末‘礼物’。”

菲扎把光盘插入电脑。不一会儿，出现了所有老师的照片。

“这样，菲扎。”比利边说边靠近她。

他离她这么近，她的脸颊都能感觉到他的呼吸，闻起来是口香糖的味儿。她不得不暗自承认他的确很帅：他有一双明澈的蓝眼睛、一头金色短发，脸上带着温和的笑容。但是，她目不斜视地盯着电脑屏幕。她害羞得不得了，都不敢直视他。

“你觉得你可以把他的头安在她的身上吗？”比利继续说。

他指着科学老师罗伯茨先生的一张照片：他戴着一副眼镜，没多少头发。接着他指了指英语老师西蒙斯女士的照片：她身材矮胖，穿着一条亮粉色连衣裙。菲扎笑了。她觉得那真是个好笑的想法。

第16页

“当然可以。”她说完就开始弄起来。

她一完成罗伯茨先生和西蒙斯女士的照片，就转向苗条美丽的历史老师布朗女士的照片。布朗女士被安上了校长的头和体育老师毛乎乎的腿。接着她又弄完了琼斯先生的照片，这位可怜的数学老师穿上了短裙，留着长长的灰胡子。

“太棒了！”比利说着，大伙儿都挤到了电脑屏幕旁。

这时他把头扭向菲扎，微笑着直视着她。

“谢了，菲扎，你真酷。”他说。

然后男孩儿们离开了教室，那些令人侧目的女孩儿们盯着菲扎看。显然她们无法相信无趣的菲扎·麦金太尔会得到帅气的比利·亚当斯如此的重视。

“哇哦！简直不敢相信！”芭布丝小声说着，坐到了菲扎身旁。

菲扎朝她回以微笑，她自己也无法相信，学校最酷的男生之一说她酷！

第17页

“菲扎！听我说！你觉得比利喜欢我吗？”芭布丝说，“他真的跟我说话了！”

“我确定他喜欢你，”菲扎说，“谁会不喜欢你呢？”

她心里笑了一下，视线转回到电脑屏幕上。

* * *

暑假第二周的一天，菲扎和妈妈去逛商场。她们在伯明翰的斗牛场购物中心。

她觉得有点儿别扭，因为她刚剪了头发。妈妈和理发师一致认为她的新发型看起来棒极了。

第18页

“就算不好，”菲扎想，“他们也肯定会那么说，不是吗？”

她真的不在乎他们怎么想，因为她心里是为了另一个人而理发的。菲扎·麦金太尔不愿向任何人承认，但她的内心有了变化。期末放假以来她每天都在卧室的镜子前看自己。

“他说我酷，”她对镜子说，“他说我酷。”

真相就是她想看起来“酷”不是为了自己，而是为了比利·亚当斯。

购物中心里到处是打发假期时间的无聊少年。她跟着妈妈走出一家鞋店，拐了个弯，迎面碰到了一群学校的男生，走在中间的就是比利·亚当斯！

菲扎能感觉到自己的脸都在发烫。她想跑开躲起来。她恨不得身处他处，只要此时此刻不是在斗牛场购物中心的此地。这时她想起了每次练柔道时爸爸跟她说的话。

“菲扎，虽然你是个女孩儿，”他说，“但那并不妨碍你和男人一样勇敢。”

第19页

于是她让自己勇敢起来。她直视比利，冲着他大大方方地微笑。

“你好，比利。”她说。

比利看了看她……然后视线移开了。

“那是谁？”菲扎听到他的一个朋友问他。

“我不知道。”比利回答。

菲扎感觉糟糕透了。比利不愿意认识她！她感觉到眼睛里有滚烫的泪水，她想要跑开，可是她不能——她得稳步走，她得显得“酷”。

“我？酷？”她想，“算了吧。”

她第一次为她要动身去萨克岛感到开心，然后她跟着妈妈快步走出了购物中心。

然而，菲扎并不知道她走开的时候，比利·亚当斯正望着她。他没有认出换了发型的她，但他觉得她是个很漂亮的女生。

第 3 章　被时间遗忘的岛

第20页

菲扎从她与父母合住的白色农舍向外边的旷野望去。她向岩石覆盖的海岸望去，然后她就看到了海岸下小型海港里整齐排成一列的小船。他们当天早些时候到达这里时，乘坐的船正开始返航回根西岛。深蓝色的海面在午后的阳光下波光粼粼，她望着那艘船在海上驶远，直到不见踪影。在她左边，可以看到一匹棕色大马向山上走来，拉着满载乘客的马车。远远地，她还看见一个男人开着拖拉机穿过田地。菲扎·麦金太尔可以看见很多景物，但是听不到任何声音。萨克岛是安静的——一片死寂。它安静得让菲扎感到不舒服。可是她的妈妈却觉得很舒服！

“这里是不是让人感到兴奋，菲扎！”鲁贝尔·麦金太尔说，她正从农舍门口走出来，在一块毛巾上擦着手。“这份宁静闻都闻得出来，不是吗？”

第21页

菲扎装作在打哈欠。“令人兴奋”是她最不想用来描述这个地方的词。她已经明白了这将是有生以来最无聊的假期。

她踢起一块石头，却不巧砸到了妈妈的脚。

“哎哟！小心点儿！你怎么这么暴躁啊，小姐？”

“对不起，妈妈。我就是累了。对不起。”

菲扎心情不好，但是她也的确累了。那天早上六点他们就从伯明翰启程了。为了赶上到根西岛的船，他们开了四小时的车。然后他们换乘了一艘更小的船到达萨克岛，一辆马车在那儿接走了他们！最后，他们到达了一户农舍，里面连电视都没有——当然也没有网络。菲扎知道这个假期完全毁了！她甚至都期盼着开学返校了！

然而，有一件事让菲扎那天开心了一点点。

早上他们的船到达的时候，迎接所有乘客的是一排马车——那是岛上的出租车服务。他们的“出租车”来自“理查德·麦金太尔马车公司”，他们的车夫是一个四十来岁的高个子男人，他一头棕色卷发，古铜色的脸上洋溢着快乐的笑容。

第23页

“你们好！我叫理查德·麦金太尔。”他说。

“我是依姆兰·麦金太尔！”菲扎的爸爸笑了，“多巧啊！”

“我们赶了这么远的路，结果竟碰到个同姓人！”妈妈说。

大家都笑了，包括菲扎，这时理查德·麦金太尔把他们的行李搬上马车，带他们赶着马车上了山。

“你们从哪儿来的呢？”他问。

“伯明翰。”

“啊，伯明翰——我猜和萨克岛有点儿不一样吧。”

“是的。那儿很大！很吵！”妈妈答道。

“那儿好得很！”菲扎想。

“那么污染情况呢？”理查德问，“在萨克岛，我们没有汽车，所以几乎没有污染！”

“哦，是的。”妈妈说，“遗憾的是伯明翰污染很严重。”

“在伯明翰我们也能做很多不错的事。”菲扎想。她从马车后面向外望去，琢磨着比利·亚当斯此刻在做什么。他没坐着那么一辆臭烘烘的马车，这点她是确定的。

第24页

“哦，你们会爱上萨克岛的！人们称它为被时间遗忘的岛。”理查德说。

“我希望我能遗忘掉它。”菲扎想。

* * *

就这样，菲扎到了这座绝对无事可做的“被时间遗忘的岛”上。恍惚中，妈妈的声音唤醒了她，她的思绪回到了眼前。

“你为什么不出去四处转转，菲扎？”妈妈说，“等你回来的时候，我就把晚饭做好了。哦！还有，请给你爸爸买份报纸。”

菲扎向山脚下的小村庄走去。只用了五分钟，她就发现了两家租自行车的商店、三家卖珠宝和水壶的商店，还有一家有超市的小邮局。菲扎走到柜台跟前。

“请问有报纸卖吗？”她问一位头发灰白的小个子老太太。

“抱歉，”她说，“还没从根西岛送过来。明天再来吧。”

“什么破地方？”菲扎想，“竟然连报纸都没有！”

她向老太太道谢后离开了商店。她开始向山上往回走时，遇到了一群和她年龄相仿的女孩子。她们嚼着口香糖，穿着短裙。她们看起来就像她的学校里那些“酷”女孩儿，这让菲扎会心一笑。

第25页

“总有些东西是不变的，”她想，“不管在哪儿。”

她拔腿往农舍跑去。

后来，吃完晚饭，菲扎和爸爸在农舍后的空地上练习了柔道。练了一个多小时，他们互相把对方摔倒在草地上，直到最后依姆兰认了输，进屋和鲁贝尔玩牌去了。

太阳像只超大的橙子，开始西沉，菲扎继续练着柔道动作。最后，她累得不练了。她望着远处深灰色的海面，深深地吸了口气。到萨克岛以来，她第一次发现自己在聆听。她可以听到鸟儿吟唱着互道晚安，还能听到远处羊儿的铃铛和船只的声音。接着，她仰起鼻子，深吸气，发现萨克岛夜晚的空气是香甜的。这和她深爱的伯明翰的浓浓的城市气味完全不同。这样的美好霎时让菲扎·麦金太尔感到充满活力，她决定表现一下，让这个岛知道她心情有多好。

第26页

“晚上好，萨克岛！”她边高高跳起边喊，然后落在草地上。

她一边嘲笑着自己犯傻，一边爬起来转身回屋，但她突然站住了。

农舍边的树上坐着一个红发男孩儿，看起来和她年纪相仿。他们俩目不转睛地互视了一会儿，然后她注意到身边跑过一只棕色小兔子。她刚错开目光，有几秒钟没看那男孩儿，他就完全消失了。

第4章　菲扎遇到弗莱彻

第27页

第二天早上，菲扎是被妈妈叫醒的。

“快点儿，懒丫头！起床了！理查德在外面，他要带我们在岛上逛逛！”

菲扎睁开一只眼，看了看手表，七点钟。“妈妈！我在度假呢！”她说着把枕头蒙到了头上。

“起来啦！理查德说这会儿是逛岛的最佳时间，等会儿人就太多了。”

“人多？这儿？”菲扎想，“看起来不太可能。”

终于，她洗完脸，刷完牙，草草吃了点儿早餐，然后出了门。妈妈、爸爸、理查德·麦金太尔和他的马车都在等她。

“早上好，小姐！”他愉快地说。

“好吗？”菲扎打着哈欠问。

“当然好了！”理查德大笑道，“太阳出来了！你准备好了吗？”

第28页

“嗯，我准备好了……”菲扎说。

她心中暗想理查德·麦金太尔是不是总是这么开心。她睡眼惺忪地爬上马车，他们的环岛旅程开始了。

接下来的几个小时，马车缓缓前行，路过了树林、田地、几间房子和几辆拖拉机，还有其他载着游客的马车。他们看见了小沙滩、海岸上的岩石和黑黑的洞，理查德说那些是岩洞。他们从德里布勒湾走到了迪克斯卡特湾，接着又走过了名为大广滩的一大片金色沙滩。大人们聊着乡村和城镇，鲁贝尔·麦金太尔跟理查德说着她从事的环境办公室职员的工作。

“我觉得伯明翰可以从萨克岛学点儿什么。”她说。

“好啊，就从摒弃所有的小汽车，然后告诉大家都去买匹马开始吧！”理查德说。

除了菲扎，大伙儿都笑了，她开始觉得坐在马车后面有些反胃。

他们继续着旅程。

“如果你们不反对，我想去维纳斯湖。那儿有片美丽的小沙滩，我儿子喜欢在那儿钓鱼。希望我们能看到他。”

第29页

他们到达小沙滩的时候，看到了一个高个子男孩儿，他穿着牛仔裤、白色T恤衫，戴着蓝色棒球帽，光着脚。他正坐在一块岩石上，身边有很多银色的大鱼。

“嘿，弗莱彻！”理查德喊道，“运气如何？”

“不错！我捉了六条大的！”

“太棒了！要不要带你一程？”

男孩儿二话没说，爬下岩石，拾起鱼，跑到了马车前。

“这是我的儿子，弗莱彻。”理查德说，“这是依姆兰、鲁贝尔……还有，不好意思，鲁贝尔——我不知道你女儿的名字！”他对菲扎的妈妈说。

“菲扎，”妈妈说，“菲扎·麦金太尔。”

“听到了吗，弗莱彻？这位小姐也姓麦金太尔！”

“所以呢？”弗莱彻无礼地说。

“弗莱彻和菲扎！两个F.麦金太尔！”理查德笑道，“你们应该很合得来。”

大人们都笑了，男孩儿面无笑容，坐到了她旁边。菲扎可以感到自己的脸因为尴尬而发烫。男孩儿把脸藏到帽子下，怀里抱着鱼。那些鱼让菲扎觉得更反胃了。她很厌恶鱼的气味。这时她注意到他没有钓竿，连渔网都没有。

第30页

“你的钓竿呢？”她问。

“我没有钓竿。”他看都没看她一眼说道。

“哦？那你怎么捉鱼？”她问。

弗莱彻只是把他脏乎乎的手举到她面前，然后就又转身背对着她了。

“他用手捉到的这些鱼？我可不信！”菲扎想，她对这个粗鲁的男孩儿立刻没有了好感。之后的旅程他们再没有说过话。

* * *

当天晚些时候，吃过晚饭，菲扎正在农舍外练习柔道，突然注意到一团黑色的影子从山上下来。等它离得近了，她认出来那是一匹毛色黑白相间的马，有人骑着它跑得飞快。她跳到一边让它过去。尽管马儿近得她都能听到它粗重的喘气声，她还是没能看清骑马人是谁，因为他脸上围着一块绿色围巾。

菲扎害怕马，特别是它们跑得那么快的时候。

“傻帽儿。”她心说，眼瞅着那个危险的骑马人跑到山下，不见踪影。

第二天，菲扎在沙滩度过了愉快的一天，傍晚练柔道的时候，她又看到了那匹黑白毛色的马。这次骑马人停在了高处的空地，似乎在俯视着农舍。他们这样停留了几秒，然后离开了。菲扎确定那是同一匹马，骑手也很有可能是同一个人。但那是谁呢？

第31页

第三天傍晚，菲扎的爸爸妈妈计划了一下晚餐。

“菲扎，我们今晚想去村子里的餐馆。”菲扎的爸爸说，“你想去吗？”

菲扎得快点儿想。她不想离开农舍，她不想错过那匹神秘的马。

“哦，谢谢，但我今晚觉得很累——我更想喝点儿汤、读读书。”

“哦，那我们都不出去了！”妈妈说。

“不，不——你们去，我没事。”菲扎立马回应。

爸妈承诺天黑前回来，她跟爸妈说了再见，然后又来到外面的空地上练起了柔道动作。这又是一个美丽的傍晚，只是过了大约一小时，太阳要下山了，菲扎开始觉得累了。这次那匹黑白毛色的马根本没有踪迹。她转身进屋，但当她经过农舍边的那棵树时，一根树枝咔嚓掉了下来，有人落下来砸到了她身上。她想都没想就把这人过肩摔到地上。

第32页

“哎呀！”

是一个高个子男孩儿，穿着牛仔裤、白色T恤衫，光着脚，戴着一顶蓝色棒球帽。帽子掉了下来，浓密的红发和绿色的眼睛露了出来，眼里透露出菲扎见过的最生气的神色。那是弗莱彻，理查德·麦金太尔的儿子！

“你！”菲扎说，“你监视我？”

“没有！”

“有，你就是！我之前晚上也看见过你！”

弗莱彻换了话题。“不说这个，你弄断我的脚腕了！”他扶着腿说道。

“我弄断了你的脚腕？你刚刚在树上！你自己摔断的脚腕！”

“哎哟！”弗莱彻又说。

菲扎蓦地为自己把他摔到地上感到有点儿愧疚。

“你觉得还能走吗？”她语气稍微温和了一些。

弗莱彻摇了摇头。

“来，你的手扶着我。我扶你起来。”

第33页

弗莱彻费力地站了起来，菲扎扶着他走进农舍，让他坐到厨房的椅子上。

“你真觉得脚腕断了？”她问，“你能动动它吗？”

她不知道自己为何问他那些，但电影里的人就是那么说的。

“还行，还能动点儿。”弗莱彻说。

“呃，要不要我叫你爸爸来接你？”

“你想叫就叫呗。”他回答。

菲扎再次被这个男孩儿的无礼惹恼了，她用手机给他爸爸打了电话。理查德·麦金太尔到的时候，菲扎的爸妈也到了。

“你干什么了，弗莱彻？”理查德笑道。

“没干什么，”弗莱彻说，“我从树上掉下来了，就是这样。现在感觉好些了。”

“来吧，我们回家。跟菲扎说谢谢。”弗莱彻的爸爸说。

“谢谢。”弗莱彻低声说，他爸爸扶着他离开了厨房。

透过窗户，在夜晚的灯光中，菲扎看着理查德·麦金太尔扶弗莱彻上马。没看错，就是那匹黑白毛色的马。

第 5 章　山上的马

第34页

第二天上午，菲扎被卧室窗外“哐”的一声巨响弄醒了。

她揉了揉眼睛，看了下手表。12 点 15 分。她怎么会睡了那么久？她的思绪被外面持续的吵闹声打断了。

“哎呀！”

“嘿哟！”

“嘿哟！”

是两个男人打斗的声音。她迅速拉开窗帘，正好看到她爸爸把理查德·麦金太尔从左肩摔下。

“啊！”理查德大喊，“我的后背！”

“你着地方法还是不正确！”她爸爸回应，“我们再来。”

“我们不先喝杯咖啡吗，依姆兰？”理查德问。

菲扎觉得他语气里满是期待。

第35页

“不！来吧！你可以的！”

菲扎暗自笑了。可怜的理查德！她知道他现在肯定有的那种感受。她爸爸一旦有了新的柔道学生，就不会轻易放他们走。

过了一会儿，菲扎走出了农舍，走到了阳光下。

“早上好，菲扎，”爸爸说，“或者我是不是该问下午好？”

“你好，菲扎。”理查德坐在草地上没动地方，抬头冲她笑着说。“萨克岛的空气让你睡得很香，对吗？”

说得对啊，她在家从来没有睡得这么香过。

“对，”她说，“弗莱彻今天在哪儿？他的脚腕儿怎么样了？”

“哦，他的脚腕儿没事！他正替我赶马车呢，所以我上午有空儿——”

“所以我就给他上上柔道课！”她爸爸说着，伸出手把可怜的理查德拉了起来。

“但我会告诉他你想见他！”理查德继续说道。

“想见谁？”菲扎说。

“弗莱彻！”

“不想，就问问！”菲扎迅速说，但太晚了。理查德已从口袋里掏出了手机。

第36页

“弗莱彻？一切还好吗？”他对着手机喊。

就在理查德听着他儿子答话的时候，菲扎努力抑制住自己大叫一声或是跑下山去的冲动。为什么这些大人总是给她难堪？她不想见那个无礼的小子！

“猜猜什么事，弗莱彻！”理查德继续道，“我和菲扎·麦金太尔一起在农舍这儿呢。你完事了过来吧？”

可怜的菲扎觉得她难堪得要爆炸了，就像她在斗牛场购物中心看到比利·亚当斯那次。

“你们俩一定要留下吃午饭！”妈妈端着两大杯咖啡从农舍出来。

“还能不能更惨点儿？”菲扎想。

午饭时，三个大人愉快地聊着，而菲扎和弗莱彻，虽然挨着坐，但是都默默地坐着，不看对方。

“谢谢你，鲁贝尔！咖喱鱼太好吃了！”理查德放下刀叉时说。

“谢谢，”菲扎的妈妈说，“这是菲扎最喜欢的，对吗，宝贝？”

第37页

菲扎做出一脸怪相，逗得弗莱彻哈哈大笑。

“至少他还找到了点儿有意思的事。”她想。

“非常感谢你们的午餐，”理查德说，“我想现在我是否可以——”

没等他说完这句话，菲扎的爸爸就腾地从桌边站起来。

“再练会儿柔道？”

“呃，谢了，依姆兰，”理查德说，“但我也有个建议。你们想不想跟我去拜访一位朋友？她住在岛的那边，会做精美的陶器。”

“太棒了！”菲扎的妈妈说。

“我更想再练会儿柔道。”爸爸说。

“依姆兰！”鲁贝尔生气地说，“我们想去。谢谢你，理查德。你想去吗，菲扎？”

菲扎想说，比起去拜访个做陶器的，她更愿意吃咖喱鱼，但是，作为一个懂礼貌的女孩儿，她保持了沉默。

“也许菲扎想和弗莱彻一起留下？”理查德说。

菲扎可以感觉到她的脸又变红了。

“弗莱彻，”他说，“要不你带菲扎去看一下我们的马？”

第38页

菲扎觉得如果她说她不喜欢马，也会显得有点儿无礼。

“她要是愿意的话，可以。”弗莱彻看都不看她一眼说道。

* * *

这两个 15 岁的孩子望着理查德·麦金太尔赶着马车载着鲁贝尔和依姆兰·麦金太尔沿着海边的路走远了。最后，马车从视线里消失了，但他们还是默默地站着。菲扎开始猜想他们是不是要这样待一下午。

“你到底想不想看马？”弗莱彻突然说。

菲扎转过脸对着他，他们还是第一次正式地看对方。

她看到一个眼睛又大又绿、鼻子上长着褐色小雀斑的男孩儿，而他看到一个眼神温暖善良、秀丽的脸庞边散着浓密的黑色卷发的女孩儿。恰在同时，他们相视而笑。

“想，很好啊。”菲扎回答。

“来吧，我们的马都养在山上的马舍里。我们走着去可以吗？”

第39页

“当然可以！”菲扎回答。

“哦，对了，我忘了。你运动能力不错——在女生里。”

“多谢夸奖。你马骑得不错——在男生里。”菲扎回答。他们笑着一起往山上跑去。

他们走进一个四方大院，菲扎四处环视。她可以看到一排木制马厩，每个马厩里都有一匹大马。

“看我的。”弗莱彻说着把嘴唇一撮，吹了个口哨儿。

马儿们立刻竖起耳朵，变得极其兴奋。看得出它们见到他很高兴。菲扎却挪到了弗莱彻身后，因为它们使她感到紧张。

“没事，菲扎，它们不会伤到你，它们很温和。”弗莱彻说，“因为要拉马车，这些马就得体型大点儿。还有三匹马今天在外面干活儿呢。”

他把手放在一匹马身上，轻轻抚摸着。菲扎看得出来弗莱彻疼爱这些马。突然，他们身后传来一阵声响。是那匹黑白毛色的马，他正踢着马厩的门。

第40页

“那是小金——他认得你！他在向你问好呢！”弗莱彻笑道。

“小金？”菲扎回答，“可他不是金色的啊，他是黑白色的！”

“是的，但别告诉他，他自己不知道！”他小声说。

第41页

菲扎大笑，接着手指向一匹鼻子是灰粉色的漂亮白马。

“别告诉我，那匹叫巧克力！”她说。

“别傻了，她叫乌云！你要不要摸摸她？”

菲扎小心翼翼地伸出手去揉了揉乌云的鼻子。她没想到那鼻子那么柔软。

“她真可爱。”菲扎说，她放松了一点儿。

“你想骑骑她吗？”弗莱彻说。

菲扎迅即把手抽开。她从来没骑过马。

“哦，不！谢谢了！不，我骑不了！我不行！”

弗莱彻朝她笑了笑。

“来吧，菲扎，”他说，“我教你。”

第 6 章　乡村牛仔

第42页

菲扎站在一块空地中央。乌云在她一侧，小金在另一侧。

“好了，”弗莱彻说，“首先，你得上马，像这样！”

他轻轻一跃，就爬上了小金的马背。

第43页

“现在，你试试。”

菲扎有些忐忑，她抓住乌云的皮带，把腿高高地甩到半空——倒霉的是，那一刻，乌云动了一下，菲扎摔到了地上。弗莱彻哈哈大笑，笑得好像都要从马上掉下来了。

“不，不，不！你不是和她较劲的！”他笑出了眼泪，说着从小金背上下来。

“来，我来帮你。”说着他伸出手扶她站起来。

菲扎因为被人嘲笑了有点儿生气，所以起初拒绝去扶他的手。

“哎呀，来吧！”他说，“扶住马鞍，左腿给我……现在把右腿抬高，过去……吁！小心！”

菲扎把腿抬到半空中时，差点儿就踢到了弗莱彻的头，但接下来发现，她骑到了乌云的背上。弗莱彻迅速回去跃到小金背上。

“好了！开始！”他说，“走吧！”

他轻轻踢了一下小金，他们便在旷野上飞奔了起来。菲扎看着他们离开时嘴都合不上了。

“他疯了吗？我可没法儿那么骑！”她想。

第44页

然而，弗莱彻一到达牧场的边缘，就调转了小金的方向，回到了她这儿。

“你怎么不跟着我？”他笑着说。

菲扎朝他摇了摇头。这家伙疯了……不过没出事。

“我不像你！我不会像牛仔那样骑马！”她说。

“我不敢相信你以前没骑过马。在伯明翰你都干什么呢？”

“我把时间花在电脑上，我练习柔道，有时候还会去斗牛场逛街。”

“斗牛场？”

“那是个购物中心。”

“你喜欢购物？”

“不算很喜欢，但我的朋友芭布丝喜欢。”

“哦，我知道了。”弗莱彻说，他无法理解如果不是为了买马粮，为何有人会喜欢购物。

“每个牛仔都要有个绰号，”他说，“那我就叫你……‘斗牛场酷妞’吧！”

接下来的两个小时里，弗莱彻·麦金太尔耐心地教着菲扎·麦金太尔如何骑马。他们开始是慢慢地让马走，逐渐地，他让菲扎骑得快一些。有一次，乌云跑得有点儿太快了，菲扎非常害怕。

第45页

“我停不下来了！”她高声叫着，“我停不下来了！”

弗莱彻迅速追上了她，抓住乌云的皮带勒住了马。他看得出来她在哭。

“没事的，没事的，菲扎。”他温和地说，“你骑得非常好，我不会让你受伤的，我保证。”

弗莱彻说到做到。他非常温和、耐心地教着菲扎如何骑马。到傍晚时，她的屁股有点儿疼，但她过得非常开心。

“谢谢你。”他们把马牵回马厩时她说。

“没什么。”弗莱彻回答，“嗯……你明天打算干什么？”

“没计划。”菲扎说，她突然害羞了，“怎么了？”

“嗯——你愿意跟我去看看萨克岛的一些秘地吗？”

“我们能骑马去吗？”

“还有别的去法吗？”弗莱彻回答。

“约好了！”

她刚一说完，就意识到不该用“约”这个字。

第46页

“我的意思是，那很好啊！”她马上解释，感觉自己脸红了。她注意到弗莱彻的脸也红了。

“好，”他说，“明天见。”

菲扎在回农舍的路上意识到自己一整天一次都没有想起过伯明翰、芭布丝和比利·亚当斯。

* * *

在接下来的一周里，菲扎和弗莱彻形影不离。他告诉她如何用手抓鱼，而她给他展示她最得意的柔道招式。他带她去看那些神奇得不得了的鱼儿乐于游嬉之地，而她在她爸爸那台老旧的文字处理器上给他演示一些小窍门。他们去爬树，还在维纳斯湖美丽清澈的水里游泳。他们骑着马在岛上四处巡看，菲扎骑马的技术也越来越好了，她都爱上了乌云这匹小白马。伯明翰好像已在几光年以外，他们的话题只有小岛没有别的……当然，他们还会谈到他们两家的家长看起来相处得很不错这件事。理查德成了鲁贝尔和依姆兰的导游，鲁贝尔成了理查德的厨师，而依姆兰则成了理查德的柔道教练——不管理查德喜不喜欢！菲扎对弗莱彻的妈妈一无所知。有一回他们往海里扔石头的时候，他只提过她一次。

第47页

“我好多年都没见过我爸爸这么开心了，自从我妈妈离开后就完全没有过了。”他说。

“那是多少年前？”菲扎问。

“太早以前了。”弗莱彻说着生气地往波浪里扔了块石头。

菲扎能感觉到他不想聊这个，所以她换了个话题。

“嗯，你可以谢谢你爸爸，因为我爸妈这个假期过得很精彩……我也是！”

弗莱彻对她笑了笑，然后跳起来。

“谁后下海谁就是坏蛋！”他说。

菲扎追着他踏进了海里，身上还穿着牛仔裤。

* * *

有一天下午，他们到一个黑暗的岩洞里探险。刚进洞的时候菲扎什么也看不到，但过了一会儿她就看到有东西在他们头顶飞来飞去。

“那些是什么？”她问。

“蝙蝠，”弗莱彻说，“它们生活在黑暗的地方。”

“啊！我讨厌蝙蝠。”菲扎说，这时正有一只黑色的小蝙蝠径直飞到她头上。她大叫起来，她的叫声吓到了蝙蝠，那蝙蝠就挂在了她头发上。

第48页

“啊！把它弄开！弄开！”她大喊。

“嘿！斗牛场酷妞怎么会害怕蝙蝠呢？应付这个应该是小菜一碟啊！”弗莱彻大笑着说。

他轻轻地伸出手把蝙蝠从她头发里捏出来，蝙蝠马上老实了，仿佛在弗莱彻的手上感觉到了安全。菲扎觉得该离开那个岩洞了。

“我觉得该吃冰激凌了。”她说。

“凡是牛仔都得吃冰激凌！”弗莱彻说。

他们笑着爬出了岩洞，然后解开了正耐心在外等候的马。

之后他们坐在海港的堤坝上吃起了冰激凌。

“你是怎么做到的？”菲扎问。

“做什么？”弗莱彻嘴里含着一大口草莓冰激凌回应道。

“你是怎么让动物信任你的？”

“我不知道，但就这样发生了。”

这时一群“酷酷的”女生走过。她们就是菲扎到这儿度假的第一天看到的那群女生。她们看看弗莱彻，接着又看看菲扎，互相嘀咕着什么，然后转过拐角不见了。

第49页

“你认识她们吗？”菲扎问。

“不算吧。她们在学校和我同班。”

他停顿了一下。

“她们觉得我很怪。”

“为什么？”菲扎问。

她突然意识到她对弗莱彻的学校生活和朋友一无所知。

“我猜，因为我另类吧。实际上，她们叫我‘乡村牛仔’。”

“你喜欢她们那样说吗？”菲扎问。

“我其实不在乎。我和动物们的聊天比他们聊的那些东西有意思多了……不过我喜欢某些人。”他补充了一句，腼腆地看着她。

菲扎感觉到她的脸又红了。

“我觉得你不能永远信任人类，”他说，“但是你可以永远信任动物。”

“甚至是疯狂的蝙蝠？”

“甚至是疯狂的蝙蝠！”

这时他的手机响了。

“嗨，爸爸！”

听着爸爸说的话，他脸上的笑容很快消失了。

第50页

“什么？您确定？……好，我马上到。”

他把手机放回衣袋，转向菲扎。他那明亮的绿眼睛因为愤怒而变得暗淡了。

“我刚说过不能信任人类吧？”

“怎么了，弗莱彻？”菲扎问。

“有两匹马被偷了。”

第 7 章　菲扎有了计划

第51页

“我无法相信，”理查德·麦金太尔说，“这种事之前从来没发生过。”

菲扎和弗莱彻站在他边上。两人都凝视着那两个空空的马厩。

“谁会偷马呢，爸爸？谁偷的？”弗莱彻气愤地问。

“他们肯定不会离得太远吧？”菲扎问，“萨克只是个小岛。”

“那得他们还在岛上。”弗莱彻说。

“嗯，你已经报警了，是吗？”菲扎说，“他们必须马上搜岛！”

“菲扎！这里不是伯明翰！”弗莱彻犀利地说。

“弗莱彻的意思是我们岛上只有一个兼职的警官。”理查德平和地插了一句。

“哦，我知道了。”菲扎说。

“那他在哪里呢？”弗莱彻问。

“我给他打电话的时候，他正在外面钓鱼——不过他正往回赶呢。”理查德回答。

第52页

之后他们听说在大一些的根西岛和泽西岛上也有马被偷了。萨克岛的那位警察来到了马舍，和理查德低声交谈了一会儿，然后打电话向根西岛警方求助。

“要命，”跟对方打完电话后他说，“他们现在很忙，但他们许诺会尽快派出援手。”

这可让弗莱彻受不了了，他生气地踢了一扇马厩门。

“那可不行！”他吼道。

“儿子，我们得耐心点儿。”理查德说。

弗莱彻走出了院子，理查德看着菲扎担忧的脸色。

“别见怪，菲扎，”他说，“弗莱彻不是有意的。只是他很爱这些马——可能比我还爱。这些马对他而言不仅仅是工作对象，它们是他的家人。”

这时，菲扎的爸爸妈妈到了。她爸爸端着一口大炖锅。

“我估计大家都想吃点儿东西了，”鲁贝尔说，“所以我给你们大家做了咖喱鱼！”

“我刚刚还以为事情最糟不过是那样了呢。”菲扎小声嘀咕了一句。

第53页

一整个下午，理查德·麦金太尔头一次笑了。

* * *

菲扎发现弗莱彻坐在一堵墙上，俯视着山下的大海，她便在他边上坐下。他们一同看着太阳从深橘色变成血红色，然后落下了海平面。终于，弗莱彻出了声，菲扎转过来看他。他的脸被泪水打湿了。

“弗莱彻，”她说，“会好起来的。我知道会的。”

“不，不会的！”他气恼地说，“从来没有变好过！我受够了总是有人夺走我身边的东西！”

“你的马会找回来的，我知道会的。”

“她就没回来。”

“谁？”菲扎问。

“她。”

他低头看着自己的手。

“妈妈。”

菲扎望着远处的海。她真不知道该说什么。她妈妈总在她身边，她不知道没有妈妈是什么样的，所以她决定安静地听弗莱彻说。他告诉菲扎，十岁那年，有一天放学回到家，他发现爸爸在厨房的餐桌边哭泣。他的大手里攥着一张字条，是他的妻子——弗莱彻的妈妈留下的。字条上说她待不下去了，她需要过远离萨克岛的生活，她需要过真正的生活。她说走就走了。那天早上，是弗莱彻最后一次看到妈妈。他父母最终离婚了，于是，过去的五年里，就只有他和爸爸……还有那些马。

第54页

“我以前从没和任何人说过这件事，”他说，“我从来都没想说。”

菲扎看着他，对他淡淡一笑。她突然觉得与任何朋友，甚至是与芭布丝相比，她和弗莱彻的关系都更亲近。

“谢谢。”弗莱彻说，他用 T 恤衫把脸上的泪水擦去。

“随时奉陪。”菲扎说。

他们对彼此微笑，然后又看向远处的海。

“有了！”菲扎突然说，“我们得把马夺回来！你猜怎么着？”

弗莱彻坐直了，用还含着泪水的大大的绿眼睛看着菲扎。

“怎么着？”他问。

第55页

“我有个计划。”

* * *

这两个 15 岁的少年在漆黑的夜空下把乌云牵到了牧场中央。这匹小马的白色皮毛在月光下闪闪发亮。

“没事的，小宝贝！”弗莱彻边把她拴在一棵小树上，边对着她的耳朵低语，“我们会看着你的。”

他们迅速回到牧场的黑暗角落，只留下马站在那里。

“我不敢看她！她看起来那么恐惧！”菲扎说。她已经开始后悔自己想出的这个把一匹马留在外面做诱饵抓偷马贼的主意了。

尽管如此，弗莱彻和菲扎还是躲在一棵大树后面看着乌云。他们选中她做此事是因为她那白亮的皮毛在几百米以外就能轻易被看见。一个小时过去了，什么也没发生，然后又是一个小时。菲扎开始感到困倦了，她的眼皮发沉了。

“弗莱彻！”她轻声说，“我们放弃吧？这主意真傻！显然没有人来偷她！”

突然，弗莱彻抓住她的胳膊。

“嘘！”他说，“看！那是什么？”

第56页

在牧场的另一边，他们看到一盏小灯。菲扎屏住了呼吸，因为它正向乌云小小的白色身影靠近。很快，他们俩都看到了那盏灯是被一个男人拎着的。

“就是他！”弗莱彻低声说。

片刻之后，那人上了马，就像他倏忽出现一样，他带着那匹小马倏忽消失在夜色中。

“可怜的乌云！”菲扎说。

“快点儿！”弗莱彻边低声说边追着他们跑上去。

他们追到了牧场边缘，顺着山势望向低处月光照耀的海面。乍一看，他们什么都没看见，但接着菲扎突然跳了起来。

“她在那儿呢！”她说。

第57页

弗莱彻向山下望去，看到正缓慢行进的白色身影，没错，就是乌云。

“快！”他低语，“注意保持距离！”

他们慢慢地、尽量无声地跟着马和劫走她的人走了差不多20分钟。他们看不出要往哪儿去，有几次他们被石头和灌木丛绊倒了。菲扎的脚开始感到疼了，她觉得很冷。她觉得要是穿件暖和些的毛衣就好了。海在他们的右边，但当他们走在几棵大树后面的时候，海就被遮住了。

“我觉得他要把她牵到德里布勒湾去。”弗莱彻说。

他们知道海就在不远处，因为他们能听到海浪击打海岸的声音。现在菲扎着急了，因为她没有想过计划奏效后下一步怎么做！

“那我们现在该做什么？”她在黑暗中跟弗莱彻小声说。

“没事，菲扎，”他说，“该我来想法子了。”

接着，他从口袋里掏出手机。

第 8 章　设个圈套

第58页

弗莱彻和菲扎悄悄地向山下又走了几米，然后躲在一片小灌木丛后小心翼翼地往外看。乌云的劫持者和另一个人在海滩上碰了面，他们正在对话。他们离菲扎和弗莱彻很近，菲扎和弗莱彻都能听到他们说话。黑暗中，他们可以看到那两个人一胖一瘦。是那个瘦子偷走了乌云。

“干得好！看起来是匹好马！”胖子说。

“是的，我们得卖个好价钱。”瘦子答道，“船什么时候到这儿？”

“随时会到……我去把别的马牵来。”胖子说。

他消失在海滩一角的几块大岩石后面。不一会儿他从黑暗中回来，牵着两匹大马。

“那是我们家的马！”弗莱彻气愤地低语，“那些人把它们藏在这儿了！”

很显然他们在等待带他们离岛的船。过了不一会儿，一盏绿灯在远处的海上闪了三次。

第59页

“嘿！有信号！他们来了！”瘦子喊道。

菲扎和弗莱彻意识到如果他们打算制止这些人，现在就得行动，来不及等援手了。

“好，菲扎，”弗莱彻低语，“我们该行动了……”

几秒钟后，菲扎在原地没动，只听弗莱彻轻轻吹了声口哨。沙滩上的三匹马都扬起了头来听，但那两个人没察觉到什么。他们一心忙着寻找他们的船。接着弗莱彻又吹了声口哨，马儿们开始兴奋地跳跃起来。这着实吓了那两个人一跳。弗莱彻每吹一次口哨，马儿们都会跳起来，直到将拴它们的绳子从那两个人手里挣脱掉。接着马儿们开始围着那两个人转圈跑了起来。

“抓住它们，蠢货！”一个人吼道。

“你来！它们太快了！”另一人回应。

这就是菲扎在等待的时机。她跑到海滩上，跳到半空中，高踢腿，把那个胖子击倒在地。

第60页

“哎呀！”瘦子喊道。他奋力跑去帮助他的同伙，但是三匹马挡住了他的路。他动不了！胖子面朝下趴着，菲扎骑在他身上，把他的胳膊扭到背后。

“啊！好痛！”他叫道。

“哼，那就别动！”菲扎回应。

她看着弗莱彻用绳子把瘦子的手脚绑住，然后向海面看去。盗马贼的船上的灯光越来越近了，这使得马儿都跑开了。

“等那船到这儿之后，我们该怎么办？”她问弗莱彻。

“对啊！”满嘴沙子的胖子说，“你们该怎么办？”

“没事，”弗莱彻说，“不会有事的。”

实际上，弗莱彻也开始有点儿担心了。然而，就在这时，他们听到了一个熟悉的声音。

“弗莱彻？是你吗？”

“爸爸！”

理查德·麦金太尔从黑暗中出现了。他后面是菲扎的爸爸依姆兰，再往后是他的两个马车夫。

第61页

“你们终于来了！”弗莱彻说，“我都开始以为您没有收到我叫您来这儿找我的信息呢！”

菲扎惊愕地看着自己的爸爸。

“爸爸？”菲扎说，“您在这儿干什么？”

“我本来觉得你可能需要我搭把手。”她爸爸答道，又看了看那个垂头丧气的胖子，“但我现在知道你终究还是从我的课上学到东西了！”

第62页

“你们找到了马！”理查德说，“太棒了！”

然后他神情严肃起来。

“弗莱彻，你为什么不早告诉我你们在做什么？”他说，“这些人会很危险的！”

那个瘦子深以为然地点着头，但是没有人理他。

“没事的，爸爸。我和菲扎控制住了局面，对吧，菲扎？”

菲扎笑了笑，这时她发现盗马贼的船已经非常近了。她还是不确定等船到达时会发生什么。船上可能有很多的同伙儿！然而，船刚一到达海滩，就被四面八方雪亮的灯光照得通明。

“不许动！我们是警察！关掉发动机！”一个声音透过扩音器传出来。

雪亮的灯光来自四艘警船，他们之前早已悄悄抵达了黑暗的水域，这完全吓住了那些盗马贼。警船包围了他们，他们无路可逃。

“好像我们萨克岛的警察叫来了根西岛的警察。”理查德说，“我打电话的时候他说他会叫他们的。”

第63页

菲扎看看弗莱彻，笑了。

“成了，乡村牛仔？”

“不错，斗牛场酷妞，”他回答，“不错。”

* * *

第二天既是个好日子也是个坏日子。好是因为菲扎和弗莱彻帮忙抓到了盗马贼，这使得他们成了当地的英雄。然而，坏是因为那是菲扎假期的最后一天。说起来真像是个玩笑——两周前她不想来萨克岛，而现在她不想离开了！

理查德·麦金太尔把他们连人带行李送到海港。菲扎难过地看着他把行李箱从马车里搬到路上。依姆兰道别时许诺说，如果理查德去伯明翰就免费给他上柔道课。然后理查德亲吻了鲁贝尔的脸颊，感谢她烹制的美味咖喱鱼。接着轮到菲扎向坐在一面墙上的弗莱彻道别了。

“代我向马儿们道别，”她这么说是因为不想向他说再见，“这段日子很精彩。谢谢。”

“是的，”弗莱彻轻声说，他没有看她，“最好的时光。”

第64页

菲扎忽地就害羞了，她难过地爬上了船。但当她转身时，他已经走了。她知道也许她再也不会见到他了。

“他不在意我要离开！”她想，“他甚至都不等到船启航！”

不过菲扎·麦金太尔并不知道真正的原因。弗莱彻·麦金太尔之所以离开，是因为又一次有人把他弃于身后，而且那个人对他来说已经有了很特别的意义。

船开启了跨海行程，菲扎的爸爸妈妈向理查德挥着手，直到他从视线里消失。这时，菲扎的妈妈转身向菲扎微笑。

“有件事你知道吗，菲扎？”她说。

这会儿菲扎难受得无法回答。

“我觉得理查德·麦金太尔马车公司可能是伯明翰某些大问题的解决办法。”

“您的意思是？”菲扎凝视着海浪问。

“等等就知道了，菲扎。等等就知道了。”

第 9 章　菲扎认了错

第65页

这是秋季学期的第一天，菲扎慢悠悠地走进学校大门。

“菲扎！”

她转过身来，看见她的朋友芭布丝正朝她跑来。

“菲扎！猜猜发生了什么！”

“什么？”菲扎问。

“我谈恋爱了！”

“和比利？”

“哪个比利啊？”芭布丝说，“不是！是我在希腊遇到的一个超棒的男生。他叫杰克，他真的很帅！我对他着了魔！”

芭布丝告诉了菲扎一切有关杰克的事，包括他是哪里人、他们如何计划尽早再见面。

“你的假期过得怎么样，菲扎？”她终于讲完了自己的事情，然后问道，“萨克岛怎么样？”

“爽，”菲扎说，“很爽。”

第66页

这时芭布丝的手机响了一下。

“哦！”芭布丝大叫，“是杰克发的短信！稍等一下！”

菲扎笑了。上学期芭布丝还疯狂地喜欢比利·亚当斯。然而，这学期她就忘了他是谁，又疯狂地喜欢上了另一个人。

* * *

这天上午，菲扎遇到了一个意外，而且还不是什么好事。全校的人都聚集在大礼堂听校长讲话。所有学生都得听着他喋喋不休，还要忍住不打哈欠。

“下面，我要说一件非常严肃的事情，是关于上学期某个很出格的行为。”

大家都坐直了听着。

“上学期末某些同学干的这事。”

他举起一张两位老师的照片。一位女老师长了胡子，穿着男士裤子，而她旁边是一位穿着黄色花朵连衣裙的男士。菲扎马上认出了那张照片。那是她帮比利·亚当斯修过的一张照片。

“计算机教室将停用，直到这个——或这些——干了这件事的人来我办公室见我。”校长说，“好了，全体同学请回班。”

第67页

菲扎挪不动身子。干这事的就是她！芭布丝瞪着大眼睛看着她，她还能感觉到那些“酷”女孩儿们在她后面窃窃私语。

“你打算怎么办？”芭布丝低声问。

菲扎知道她要做什么。

“我得去见校长。”她说。

“那比利·亚当斯呢？那是他的主意！”芭布丝说。

“但是图片是我做的，”菲扎说，“待会儿见。”

她离开了学校礼堂，去校长办公室门外等着。

* * *

校长透过眼镜框上部看向菲扎。他桌子上放着菲扎修过的那些老师的照片。

“这事最不可能是你干的啊，费莉西蒂。你为什么做这种事？”

“我不知道。我当时觉得很搞笑，我估计。”

校长摇了摇头，显然他很诧异。

第68页

“这些照片全是你一个人做的？”

菲扎顿了一下。她不打算说出比利·亚当斯的名字，即使那是他的主意。

“是的，先生。”她强忍着不哭说道。

“嗯，那样的话——”校长刚一开口，就被敲门声打断了。

是校务助理。

“我把比利·亚当斯带来了。他想见您。”

比利·亚当斯走进办公室时，菲扎意识到自从假期在斗牛场购物中心那天起就没再见过他了。他被夏日的阳光晒黑了，他的金发长了些，而且现在几乎成了白色。菲扎觉得他看起来比以前更帅了。

“你好，比利。有什么事吗？”校长问。

“先生，那是我的主意。”他说，“计算机恶作剧全是我的主意。”

他直视前方站立着，一眼都没看菲扎。

“但是，”校长说，“费莉西蒂说全是她一个人干的。”

“哦，她说的不对，先生。那是我的主意。”比利回答。

第69页

“这家伙真够仗义的，”菲扎想，“他要把整件事的责任揽过去！”

实情是比利·亚当斯觉得愧疚了。跟老师开这玩笑是他的主意，如果这个文静的女生因此陷入麻烦，那是不公平的。校长听着比利解释这件事的原委。

“比利，我明白这是你的主意，但是费莉西蒂也不应该帮你，”校长说，“你们俩都有错。”

然而，校长暗自对他们的诚实品质感到欣慰。他让他们给照片上涉及的所有老师写一封道歉信。

“好了，回班里去吧。如果这学期再有什么不良表现，你们就麻烦了。”

到了外面的走廊里，菲扎正准备走开，比利叫住了她。

“谢谢你，”他说，“你没必要把责任揽过去。”

“不，有必要，”菲扎说，“我也参与了。”

比利仔细看了一下菲扎。他无法相信这是那个上学期末帮他修照片的那个女生。她如此不同！她那么自信！而且，他之前没有发现她这么漂亮！

第70页

* * *

菲扎放学回到家时，妈妈正在厨房等她。她看起来很严肃。

“嗨，菲扎，”她说，“我今天接到了一个电话……”

“哦，不要啊。”菲扎想，“一定是校长打的！现在妈妈肯定要跟我生气了！”

“我不得不说——”妈妈说。

菲扎等着被训。

“——有件激动人心的事很快就会在伯明翰发生了！但还得保密！最终确定下来之前我不能告诉你！”

接着妈妈在厨房里欢欣雀跃。

“什么事啊？”菲扎笑着问。

“哦，我不能告诉你！我真希望能告诉你，但是这是议会事务，得公事公办！”

“一点儿都不能说吗？”菲扎问。

“好吧。”妈妈说，“我说两个词：马，还有马车！”

接下来不管菲扎再问多少问题，妈妈都不肯透露更多了。

“对了，”她转移了话题，“你返校第一天过得怎么样啊？”

菲扎正思量着要不要告诉妈妈那件惹怒校长的麻烦事，这时电话响了。

第71页

“我来接！”她说着跑去接电话。

“喂？”她说。

“是菲扎吗？”是一个男孩儿的声音。

“什么事？”

“菲扎，我是比利。比利·亚当斯。”

菲扎的心扑通猛跳了一下。

“哦，你好，”她说道，尽力让自己的声音听起来冷静。

“我想问你是否愿意来公园。”

“什么时候？”

“今天傍晚？”

一个小时后，菲扎发现自己正和比利·亚当斯在公园散步。这是多么不可思议的一天啊！这一天以难受的感觉开始，却以美好的感觉收尾！他们边走边聊着学校、家人和朋友。他告诉她他多么热爱踢足球和弹吉他，她跟他聊着她学的柔道。

“那给我做个招式看看吧！”比利说。

于是菲扎给他一个背摔，把他摔倒在地上，这让他俩笑了好一会儿。

“你是从哪儿学的？”他躺在草地上问。

第72页

“我爸爸教我的！”菲扎笑道。

“那跟他说我也想上几节课吧！”

接着他们聊起了暑假，菲扎跟他讲了她在萨克岛上的奇遇，关于那些马和弗莱彻的。“这么说那算不算假日恋爱啊？”比利问。

菲扎笑起来。

“不算！当然不算！他只是个特别好的朋友！”

第73页

天色开始变暗了，比利送她回家。

“你还想这样吗？”到她家门口时，他问道。

“想。这样挺好的。”她回答。

“明天晚上怎么样？你有时间吗？”

“好，我有时间。”她说。

一刹那，她在萨克岛的假日好像已经过去很久了。

第 10 章　一名新生

第74页

两个星期后的一天，菲扎走进校门。

“菲扎！”

她转身看见芭布丝向她跑来。

“菲扎！是真的吗？”

“什么真的？”

“你在和比利·亚当斯约会？”

菲扎大笑起来。

“什么？没有！当然没有！他只是个朋友。”

“嗯。”芭布丝说。

显然芭布丝不相信她。

开学以来这两周，菲扎经常和比利在一起。他们去过公园、电影院，他甚至去过她家，她爸爸还教了他一些柔道招式。但他们没有牵过手或亲过嘴！她在他面前不再腼腆，但他们不是男女朋友，他们只是普通朋友。

“你知道学校人人都在议论你们吗？”芭布丝说。

第75页

菲扎确实知道。她注意到那些“酷”女孩儿们窃窃私语，但她尽量对她们视而不见。

“让她们说去吧！”菲扎大笑着说。

芭布丝没有笑，因为尽管假期遇到了杰克，她还是有点儿嫉妒菲扎和比利的关系。毕竟，是她先说喜欢他的！

* * *

菲扎因为得去图书馆还一些书，所以迟到了。她一走进教室门就惊讶地停住了，因为在前排的一张桌子那儿，坐着一个红发碧眼、有雀斑的男孩儿。是弗莱彻·麦金太尔。

“你好，菲扎。”他说。

一开始菲扎说不出话，她就张着嘴站在那儿。这肯定就是妈妈的“秘密”！

“弗莱彻？”她说，“你怎么在这儿？”

一瞬间，所有的“酷”女孩儿们都开始窃窃私语。接着老师叫菲扎坐下，然后开始上课。

课间休息时，菲扎和弗莱彻坐在操场的一个角落聊天。弗莱彻解释说他爸爸获得了伯明翰城市议会提供的工作。

第76页

“你的意思是我妈妈给他介绍了一份工作！”菲扎说。

“我猜是的。”弗莱彻说。

“是什么工作？”

“是一种‘绿色’出租车服务。”他解释道，“他把马匹和马车从萨克岛带来了。”

菲扎有一百个问题要问。

“你们住在哪里？乌云来了吗？马在哪里呢？”

弗莱彻解释说他爸爸在伯明翰租了一栋有马舍的房子。

“我们真的很幸运能租到那栋房子，”他说，“据说隔壁有个开工厂的男的也想要那块地。他想在那儿扩建还是干什么。”

“所以你们把乡村带到城市来了！”菲扎笑道，“好了，你带我看过了萨克岛的秘地，现在轮到我带你看看这所学校的秘地了！”

于是那天上午，菲扎带着弗莱彻在学校里到处转，当她带他看到那些完全不一样的教室和走廊时，他那大大的绿眼睛瞪得更大了。她看到他惊羡地盯着每一个地方。当一群群学生换教室经过他时，他跳到一边让开路，她笑了起来。

第77页

“这学校的人比整个萨克岛的人都多！”他低声说。

菲扎把弗莱彻介绍给她的朋友们。她告诉他们她认识的人当中没有谁比他对乡村和动物知道得更多了。他超棒！然而，不是所有人都像菲扎那样想。

“他是谁？”芭布丝低声说，想着他需要好好理一下头发。

“他是我在萨克岛认识的朋友！”菲扎说。

“他是不是有点儿……”

“什么？”

“你知道的……奇怪。”芭布丝说，“每次有救护车经过学校时他都会跳起来！”

“你不了解他！”菲扎说。

“他从哪儿弄来的鞋子？好难看！”

“哦，别说了，芭布丝！”

菲扎想起了他骑马、用手捉鱼和爬最高的树的样子。芭布丝不知道弗莱彻多有本事，因为她没见过他做这些事！

放学铃声响起时，弗莱彻问菲扎傍晚时候要不要去看马。

第78页

“太想了！”菲扎说。

理查德·麦金太尔在学校门口等着接弗莱彻，他向菲扎挥了挥手。菲扎觉得在学校外看到马车真有意思。

“待会儿见！”弗莱彻说着高兴地跑到他爸爸那儿，登上了马车。菲扎突然察觉到别的学生正在嘲笑他。她班上的一些女生，包括芭布丝，走过她身边。

“‘马仔’是你的兄弟吗？”一个人问。

“不是，怎么了？”菲扎说。

“嗯，你们都姓麦金太尔。”

菲扎没有回答。

“我看他是她的男朋友！”芭布丝说，她们大笑着走开了。

菲扎看着她们走了。芭布丝怎么了？为什么她也这么不友善？

* * *

后来，菲扎正准备去看弗莱彻和马舍里的马时，门铃响了。菲扎开了门，发现比利站在台阶上。

“嗨，菲扎。你准备好了吗？”他说。

第79页

“准备好什么呢？”

“去看电影呀！我们上周定好的！我买了票了！”他说。

“哦，对啊！当然了！”菲扎撒了谎。她完全忘了。

当她跑去拿外套时，她希望弗莱彻不会介意她今晚没去马舍的事。

* * *

第二天，菲扎跑进学校时感到极度愧疚。

她看到弗莱彻正坐在操场的一角看书。

“弗莱彻！对不起我昨晚没去马舍。我有好多作业。”她撒谎道。

“没关系。”他说。

"也许我今晚可以来?"

"你要是想来的话。"他说完就继续看书了。

之后，课间休息时，菲扎试图再和弗莱彻说说话，这时比利来了。

"嗨，菲扎。"他说。

"弗莱彻，这是比利。比利，这是弗莱彻，来自萨克岛。"她说。

"嗨，弗莱彻。"比利说。

但是弗莱彻没理他，把头扭开了。菲扎看着他。他的行为就像她在萨克岛第一次看到他时那样：没有礼貌，脾气不好，不招人喜欢。不像比利。前一晚她和比利在电影院过得很开心——她一直如此。

第80页

"昨晚的电影是不是很搞笑?"比利说。

弗莱彻扭过脸来生气地盯着菲扎。现在他知道了她没去马舍的真正原因。菲扎勉强朝他微笑，但他冲着一棵树走过去，爬上去坐在了他能找到的最高的树枝上。

"他没事吧?"比利说，"他有点儿——"

"什么?"菲扎语气凌厉地回应道。

"你知道的……怪?"比利说，他不喜欢菲扎跟这个古怪的男生交往。他为什么不能回萨克岛去?

"他才不怪!"菲扎说，"他很有本事！他刚到这儿，仅此而已!"

与此同时，别的学生已开始嘲笑这个新来的爬到树上去的红发男孩儿。当学校的猫爬上去和他坐在一起时，他们笑得更欢了。

"可怜的弗莱彻!"菲扎想，"我昨晚应该去看他的！整个伯明翰他谁都不认识！我算什么朋友?"

第81页

放学时，菲扎看到弗莱彻走出校门。他看起来不怎么高兴。

“弗莱彻！等等！”

但他继续走着。

“弗莱彻！我待会儿想去马舍，可以吗？”她边说边跑到他身边。

“想去就去，不过你不用和你的男朋友约会吗？”他说。

菲扎猛然意识到弗莱彻嫉妒了。

“不，我不约会，他也不是我男朋友，傻子！”她回答时比利·亚当斯正路过他们。

“嗨，菲扎。”比利故意背对着弗莱彻说。“你待会儿做什么？”

“与你无关。”弗莱彻插话道。

“我没跟你说话，乡巴佬！”比利回答。

这下弗莱彻可受不了了，他跳到了比利身上，开始使劲儿地揍他。比利踢他还击。没等菲扎弄明白发生了什么，两个男孩儿已经打成一团。

“别打了！”菲扎说，“求你们了！”

然而，他们继续厮打着，于是她抓住比利的左臂，扭到他背后，把他从弗莱彻那儿拽开了。接着她用最拿手的踢腿招式给了弗莱彻一记，把他踹倒在地。

第82页

“啊！”比利说。

“哎哟！”弗莱彻大喊。

“我说了‘别打了！’”菲扎说着就离开了。

为什么她不能同时喜欢两个男孩子呢？她心里真的没选过吗？几个月来，甚至多年以来，菲扎·麦金太尔都没有遇到过什么大事。

现在一下子该来的事都来了，她想不清楚自己是否喜欢这样。

第 11 章　坏邻居和好朋友

第83页

弗莱彻和菲扎在伯明翰市中心下了公交车。他们周围尽是高楼大厦，还有一辆辆卡车、公交车和小汽车排着队从他们身边开过。

“那么，它们在哪儿呢？”为了盖过交通的嘈杂声，菲扎大声喊着。

“什么？”

“马厩！它们在哪儿？”

“就在那边！”弗莱彻指着一堵难看的灰色墙面大声喊着，墙面中间有一扇旧木门。菲扎正好能看到那一边的马厩棚顶和一间小石屋。马舍隔壁是一家大工厂，屋顶上写着红色的“斯库利废品厂”几个字。工厂的几辆卡车就停在边上。菲扎算得上一个地道的城市女孩儿，但连她也没料到这个。对她而言，马舍应该在乡村中间，就像萨克岛的马舍那样。在市中心看到它们感觉有点儿不可思议。

第84页

“你在开玩笑吧！”她说，“你肯定不喜欢这儿！”

“进去就好了，”弗莱彻说，“来吧。哦，求你别提打架的事——爸爸会气疯的。”

“只要你别告诉我妈妈我也参与了！”她回答，“她要来这儿跟我碰头。”

弗莱彻微笑着打开了大木门，他们踏进了院子。他说得对，一进到墙这边，就不会感觉和萨克岛的马舍有那么大的区别了。菲扎第一眼看到的是一排马厩，每一间马厩里有一匹马。它们脸上还是透露着友善的表情，跟她在萨克岛度假时喜欢的样子一样。它们都转过来打招呼。这时菲扎听到有一匹马在踢马厩的门。

“我知道是谁！”她说。

她猜对了，因为在院子的一角有一匹英俊的黑白毛色的马。

“你好，小金！”菲扎笑着走到他跟前。接着她看到了乌云，便跑过去抚摸她的鼻子。

“哦！乌云！再次看到它们真好！”她喊道。

“是啊，它们也觉得再见到你很好。”弗莱彻说。

第85页

这时，弗莱彻的爸爸从房子里走出来，菲扎的妈妈跟在后面。他们都端着茶杯。

“是菲扎·麦金太尔小姐啊！救了我的马的柔道小家伙！”他大声说。

菲扎笑了。她真的很喜欢弗莱彻的爸爸，他总是那么乐呵。

“是理查德·麦金太尔先生啊！给伯明翰带来一点儿萨克岛风格，让它更环保的人！”她回应道，“您的出租马车业务怎么样？”

“哦，才刚刚开始，不过很有希望会发展得不错！”理查德说。

“我想一定会很成功的！”菲扎的妈妈说，“今天在学校过得怎么样？”

“很棒！”菲扎和弗莱彻一起撒了谎。

“你有没有交到很多新朋友，弗莱彻？”理查德问。

好在弗莱彻还没来得及回答爸爸的问题，就被几架发动机的轰鸣声打断了。斯库利废品厂的卡车全都同时发动了。接着司机开始一遍遍地按响喇叭。还是头一回，菲扎看到理查德·麦金太尔生气了。

“他们为什么一直那么干？”他问，“这一个小时里他们已经干了四次了。他们会吓坏马的！”

第86页

“我跟你说过，理查德，”菲扎的妈妈说，“是罗伯特·斯库利。他是这个工厂的老板，他很恼火市议会把这片地给了你却没给他。他想得到他想要的东西！他已经向议会控诉。他会消停的，我确定。”

乌云晃着脑袋。这匹可怜的马一点儿也不喜欢这些噪声。突然，他们看到一个矮个子男人站在大门口。他一头灰发梳到脑后，露出一张红红的脸，身上穿着一套棕色西服。

“抱歉，麦金太尔。是不是我的卡车噪声太大了？”

菲扎和弗莱彻立马知道他是谁了。他就是罗伯特·斯库利。

“嗯，它们确实吓着那些马了——”理查德开口说。

“对不起了！我的司机们有时候会很顽皮！”斯库利说完就大笑着走开了。

菲扎和弗莱彻交换了一下眼色。他们一点儿也不喜欢罗伯特·斯库利。

* * *

第二天早上，菲扎遇到了弗莱彻，他正从停在校门外的公交车上下来。

“嗨，菲扎。”他说。

第87页

“嗨，弗莱彻。罗伯特·斯库利的卡车昨晚又弄噪声了吗？”

“没有。但我们听到卡车今天一大早就全都出去了。”

“嗯，妈妈很可能是对的——他很快会消停下来。”

“对，希望如此。”

他们走进大门时，看见比利 · 亚当斯正从对面走来。

“哦，不会吧，看那是谁。”弗莱彻说。

“哦，弗莱彻，你不能试着和他做朋友吗？”

“我不想成为他的朋友。”弗莱彻回答。

“我觉得你们俩会合得来的。他人不错，真的。”

弗莱彻顿了一下，看着她。

“好吧，”他说，“我试试吧，就为了你。”

菲扎朝弗莱彻笑了笑。她明白这对他来说肯定很为难，尤其因为他是新来的。不一会儿，比利 · 亚当斯走到了拐角处，弗莱彻正等着他。

“呃，嗨，比利。”他开口说。

比利停了下来。他手里拿了块饼干，正嚼着。

“有事？”他说。

第88页

“我就是想为上次跟你打架的事说声抱歉。”弗莱彻说。

然而，弗莱彻意识到比利没有看他，因为他的目光正越过他盯着别处。弗莱彻开始发觉难以保持耐心了。

“听着，比利，我现在在尽力对你友好，但如果你不想……”

比利一句话也没说，拔腿就朝学校跑去。

“我没那么吓人吧，是吗？”弗莱彻问菲扎，她也同样很惊讶。

这时，一只大黑狗从他们身边跑过去。但它没有从比利身边跑过去——它在追他。

“你觉得它是不是在追比利手里的饼干?”菲扎问。

“我不知道——不管是追什么，它看起来可没什么善意!”弗莱彻说着扔下书包去追那只狗。

比利跳上了一堵墙，沿着上沿儿跑，但那条暴躁的狗在墙边跟着跑。比利被逼得无路可走了。狗抬头盯着他，露出牙齿，开始咆哮。它一点儿也不喜欢可怜的、吓坏了的比利。

“别怕，比利!”弗莱彻小声说，“把饼干扔到地上!”

第89页

比利迅速把吃了一半的饼干扔到草地上。狗吃了饼干，但似乎仍旧对比利感兴趣。

此时，一群学生已经聚过来兴致勃勃地围观。弗莱彻慢慢弯下腰，轻柔地叫着那只狗。

“这里，小家伙!”

狗转身开始向弗莱彻那边移动。有那么一刻，它好像也要攻击他。

“好了，小家伙，过来……”弗莱彻温和地说。

忽然，狗耷拉下耳朵，低下头，朝弗莱彻走过去。

“乖乖!”弗莱彻说着紧紧抱住了狗，“真乖!”

比利一知道自己安全了，就从墙上跳了下来。

“谢谢你，弗莱彻。”他轻声说。

“没什么。”弗莱彻回答。

菲扎过来加入了他们。

“对啦，”她说，“我们重新开始，好不好?”

两个男孩儿笑起来。

“比利，这是弗莱彻。弗莱彻，这是比利。”她说。

第90页

“嗨，弗莱彻。”比利微笑着说。

“嗨，很高兴认识你，比利。”弗莱彻回答。

第 12 章　给麦金太尔的留言

第91页

很快，弗莱彻·麦金太尔解救被疯狗缠住的比利·亚当斯的故事就成了全校的热点新闻。弗莱彻成了英雄。

弗莱彻跟比利和他的朋友们一起参加了一场足球赛，菲扎兴致勃勃地观看。

连芭布丝也突然间变得对弗莱彻很感兴趣，她一整节数学课都在问他关于他的马的事。

“真有意思！”她听他讲了他父亲的新式出租车服务时说，“我想去看看。”

菲扎听着他们的对话。芭布丝本来压根儿就不喜欢马！之后她又听到一些别的女生谈论他。

“他有点儿帅。”一个女生小声说。

“是啊，”她朋友回答，“不过他要是穿得好些的话会更好看！”

“哦，姐妹们，我们今晚是不是该带他去逛街？”芭布丝向她们喊道。

第92页

“好啊！”

“你没问题吧，弗莱彻？”芭布丝透过那她美丽的长睫毛看着他问。

“嗯，没问题。当然可以！”弗莱彻微笑道。

“我们能坐一驾你爸爸的出租马车吗？”

“好！”

放学的时候，菲扎看着弗莱彻、芭布丝和另外两个女生兴奋地登上了理查德·麦金太尔的一辆马车。芭布丝甚至都没问问菲扎是否想一起去！菲扎霎时觉得很孤独，而且意识到她嫉妒了。她说不清她是在嫉妒芭布丝，还是在嫉妒弗莱彻不跟她一起也很开心这件事。

“这不公平！”她想，“弗莱彻·麦金太尔是我的朋友！”

马车离开时，弗莱彻看到她正站在校门口，便站了起来。

“菲扎！你不来吗？”他大喊。

“不了，谢谢！我有更有趣的事要做！”她回答。

“她有‘更有趣的事要做’，弗莱彻！”芭布丝用搞怪的声音说着，并把他拽回来坐下。

第93页

菲扎不敢相信芭布丝这么小心眼儿地对待她！她难过地看着马车载满欢声笑语的幼稚女生们和弗莱彻驶开了。然而，还没等他们走远，菲扎就意识到是自己犯傻了。弗莱彻现在在学校很开心，她应该高兴才是。

“别那么自私了，菲扎·麦金太尔！”她心想。

她决定稍后到马舍去找他。

* * *

喝完下午茶，菲扎到了马舍，却发现墙上的大门没关严。她在院子外面停住了脚步。

“嗨！有人在吗？是我！菲扎！”她喊道。

里面没有回应，于是她轻轻把门推开得更大了些。她发现有几个马厩空着，有几辆马车不在。

“理查德的出租马车生意今天很忙。”她想。

随后她往院子里面看去。没有弗莱彻的影子，他可能还在外面和女孩儿们逛街。她怀疑弗莱彻是否玩儿得开心，想到这儿她笑了。接着她突然笑不下去了，因为她察觉到有什么东西不对劲，非常不对劲。她迅速扫视了一圈所有的马厩，眼前所见让她难受。每扇门上都有用红色油漆写的字。

第94页

“滚出去！”

“滚回萨克岛！”

“走……不然这匹马会成为菜单上的一道菜！”

菲扎把手放到嘴上，瞪着那些字。太可怕了！

“天哪！”她想，“希望马没事！”

第95页

她快速从一个马厩跑到另一个马厩，看到乌云、小金和其他马都还安在。接着她用手机给弗莱彻打电话。几声铃响后他接了电话。

“菲扎！你应该过来！她们想让我穿粉色衣服！”他大笑道。

菲扎能听到有女孩子在他身后大笑。

“弗莱彻。你得回马舍来。现在！”

那边停顿了一下。

“怎么了？”他问，他的声音突然变得严肃起来。

菲扎深吸了一口气。

“有人给你们留了字。”

* * *

第二天放学后，菲扎、弗莱彻和比利坐在她家花园议论着马舍发生的事。

“爸爸真的很难过。”弗莱彻说。

“我不意外！但他没想离开伯明翰吧？”菲扎问。

“我不知道。他担心的是，如果这种事再发生马会受到伤害。”

“那么，你觉得是罗伯特·斯库利吗？”菲扎问。

“不是觉得，我知道就是罗伯特·斯库利，或者是他厂里的人。”弗莱彻说。

第96页

“但警方说没证据能表明是他干的。”

“斯库利不是什么好人，”比利说，“我爸爸几年前给他当过司机。”

“我想对斯库利做点儿什么。”菲扎说。

他们都坐着思考了一会儿。

“要不我们去他的卡车上写东西？”比利建议。

“不，”菲扎说，“我们可以做点儿更有用的。”

“哦，是吗？”弗莱彻说。

菲扎点了点头。

“你爸爸是怎么看斯库利的，比利？”她问。

“他讨厌他。他认为斯库利有秘密——但还没等他弄清是什么秘密，斯库利就把他开除了。”比利答道。

“嗯，那我们去弄清吧！”菲扎兴奋地说。

“我们要怎么做呢？”比利问。

“斯库利行动！”菲扎回答。

几个小时后，菲扎和两个男孩儿制订出了一个计划，菲扎将计划打印到了一张纸上。上面写着：

斯库利行动

时间：星期二 8 点

第97页

1. 斯库利将在他家接受“校园杂志”的采访，谈谈他是如何成为伯明翰一名成功的工厂老板的
2. 弗莱彻和比利将搜查斯库利的办公室
3. 菲扎将查阅斯库利的电子邮件以发现秘密

门铃响了，菲扎跑去开门。她发现来的是芭布丝，捧着一大盒巧克力。

“哦，你好，芭布丝。”菲扎说。

自从芭布丝前一天带弗莱彻购物后，这两个女孩儿一直都没有说过话。芭布丝拿起一张纸开始念。

“菲扎，我最近对你不友好。我之前嫉妒你和比利，后来又嫉妒你和弗莱彻。没有我你好像也能过得很开心，所以我努力想让弗莱彻放弃你转而喜欢我。但我现在觉得很难过——”

“好啦，芭布丝！没关系！”菲扎打断了她。

然而，芭布丝还没说完。

“我伤心了，因为杰克不给我打电话了。他和别人好了！对不起。”

菲扎向芭布丝伸出双臂。

“哦，芭布丝，进来吧！”她说，“我给你找了个活儿。”

* * *

起先，芭布丝对去斯库利家采访他心里没谱。

第98页

“可是为什么是我去采访他？”她问。

“因为我们需要他不在场，那样我们就可以搜查他的工厂了。”菲扎回答。

“可我没在校园杂志工作！”芭布丝说。

“他不会知道这事的。”弗莱彻说。

“但我……我做不来那种事的！”芭布丝说。

“芭布丝。”比利说着把手放到她胳膊上对她笑了笑。他的金发在周日下午的阳光下闪着光，他看着比以往更帅了。“你当然可以的——因为你是最棒的。”

芭布丝看着他，脸变得有点儿红了。

“哦，那好吧。”她说。

第 13 章　斯库利怕镜头

第99页

周二晚上，菲扎在卧室电脑前坐了两个小时。她一直在尝试进入斯库利办公室的电脑，以便阅读他的邮件。然而，她就是找不到他的密码。手机响了，是芭布丝。

“菲扎！”芭布丝低声说，“我把自己锁在罗伯特·斯库利家的卫生间了！你进到他的电脑没？”

“还没有！你别让斯库利闲着！采访进行得怎么样了？”

“哦！他真的很自恋！”芭布丝说，“他已经说了两个小时他是多么有钱、他有多少辆车……还有他妻子真让人恶心！她的一切都是假的！她的头发、她的指甲，可能还有她的牙齿！她的裙子也太短了——她和我妈一个年纪了，我的老天！她到哪儿都带着一只小傻狗——”

菲扎突然打断了她。

第100页

“它的名字是什么？”

“哦……泡泡糖，就是这个。这名字也傻。”

菲扎输入了“泡泡糖”这几个字。她立刻进入了罗伯特·斯库利的电子邮箱。

“芭布丝，你真棒！”

“哦，是吗？”芭布丝说，“谢谢。”

菲扎开始在罗伯特·斯库利的电脑里浏览起电子邮件。她以前从没干过这种事，她很害怕。她要是被发现了怎么办？她会惹上斯库利这个大麻烦的。还会惹上警察！她知道她得快些。

“好了，芭布丝！你得让他一直说——我在他的电脑上，可不希望他靠近电脑！”

“哦，我不用费心跟他聊——他现在正和警察通电话呢。”

菲扎立刻停下了电脑上的工作。

“警察？为什么？”

“哦，他们给他打电话，因为好像有些盗贼闯入了他的工厂还是什么的。”

“警察抓到他们了吗？”

“我不知道——我关心这个干吗？”芭布丝说。

第101页

“因为‘盗贼’可能就是弗莱彻和比利。”

“哦。”

然而，就在她结束了和芭布丝的通话后，菲扎的手机立马又响了。是弗莱彻。

“弗莱彻？”她说，“芭布丝说警察给斯库利打电话了！你们没事吧？”

“没事……不过差一点儿！我和比利正好在警察到达的时候出来了！”

“你们找到什么了吗？”她问。

“找到了！几罐红色油漆！”弗莱彻说。

菲扎边听边在电脑前浏览着斯库利的邮件。

“你进入到斯库利的电子邮箱了吗？”弗莱彻问。

“进入了！”菲扎回答。

“怎么样？你找到什么了吗？”

“哦，找到了，弗莱彻·麦金太尔。我想我刚刚找到了。”

* * *

第二天晚上，菲扎和弗莱彻骑着小金和乌云离开了伯明翰的中心地区。很快高楼大厦就看不到了，周围的绿色更多了。

“再跟我说说那封电子邮件里说了什么。”弗莱彻说。

第102页

“那封电子邮件是写给他的全体司机的。邮件上说如果其他的垃圾场都满了，他们得把所有的垃圾都运到帕克山地区——在夜里。”菲扎回答。

“这么说他不想让任何人看到他做那事？”

“对，因为他在做违法的事！他没有把垃圾倒到合适的地方！”

“而且他还因此获利。怪不得他是百万富翁！”弗莱彻说。

“所以我们得趁他正在实施那事时逮住他！”菲扎说着从口袋里掏出一部新手机。

“什么？用手机？”

“是的，这是我妈妈的新手机，用它录像很不错！”

“你妈妈知道你拿了它吗？”

“不知道。她也不会知道的，因为我之后会把它放回去。我只是借用一下。”

最后他们到了一个大门前，上方挂着一个标牌，标牌上写着：“帕克山——绿色伯明翰之心脏。”

顺着大门，他们来到了一大片开阔的绿地，周围全是高大的树木。菲扎和弗莱彻骑着马迅速来到树底下藏了起来。他们不知道要等多久，但他们希望那天晚上斯库利的某一辆卡车能出现。

第103页

* * *

天色越来越暗了，弗莱彻突然摇了摇菲扎的手臂。菲扎睁开眼睛。他们等了那么久，她肯定是睡着了。

“看！”他小声说。

菲扎顺着弗莱彻指的方向看去。在昏暗的光线里，她影影绰绰能看到一辆大卡车的外形。它慢慢驶过那片开阔的绿地。

“他们来了！”

不会看错的，那是斯库利的一辆卡车。菲扎飞快地从口袋里掏出妈妈的手机，举起来按下“录像”按钮。卡车停下了，后车厢升起到半空中，一大堆垃圾被倾倒在了地上。

“录到了!”菲扎说。

这时手机突然响了。

“关掉!”弗莱彻低声说,“他们会听到的!”

菲扎看看手机,上面显示电话来自“家里”。

“好的!”菲扎回答,不过这时她决定接电话,以防有紧急事件。

第104页

“喂?”她说。

“菲扎?是你吗?你拿我手机在干什么呢?”

是妈妈!

“妈妈!对不起!我现在不方便说话!我待会儿打给你!”

第105页

她按下了“关机”键。现在妈妈知道她拿了手机!

“我惹麻烦了。”她想。

但当她听到卡车司机的叫喊声时,她意识到他们惹了更大的麻烦。

“谁在那儿?”

“两个小孩儿!”

“快!”弗莱彻说,“回到马那儿去!”

他们跑到小金和乌云等着他们的那棵树下。

“跟着我!”弗莱彻边说边跳上小金的背,骑着马穿过草地。菲扎告诉自己要勇敢,她努力跟着弗莱彻。他们经过卡车时,三个大汉从暗处出现,开始向他们跑过来。

“加油,宝贝儿,”菲扎对乌云说,“我们可以做到的!”

当大汉们伸手来拽她时,乌云猛地跃起。菲扎差点儿被甩到地上，但她成功挺住了。接着小马迈开腿以最快的速度穿过空地，奔到了路上。

“我们甩掉他们了！”菲扎说。

“太棒了！”弗莱彻喊道。

第106页

终于，他们觉得安全些了，便骑得稍慢了点儿。弗莱彻转过身，发现菲扎快要停住了。

“你没事吧，菲扎？”他问。

“没事。我在想法给芭布丝发个短信。”她说。

这让弗莱彻很生气。

“为什么女孩子总得互相发短信呢？不管发生什么。”他说。

“因为我们需要一个计划！”菲扎说。

就在这时，他们听到了发动机的声音从身后传来。菲扎转身去看，差点儿弄掉了手机。

第107页

“好险！”她想，“妈妈会气疯的！”

车子驶近了，他们看到是那辆垃圾卡车。它在追着他们！

“说真的，我们现在需要计划一下了！”弗莱彻说。

他踢了踢小金，让他跑得更快，而菲扎紧跟着他，开始想念家中舒适温暖的被窝。他们拼命疾驰过伯明翰的街道。他们驾着马沿着主路奔驰，再沿着窄些的街道行进，绕过环岛，又穿过桥底。但卡车就是一直跟着他们。突然，一辆夜班公交车出现，那使得小金跳了起来，弗莱彻差点儿摔到地上。最后小金将他们带到一条窄得卡车过不去的小道上，卡车无法再跟上了。在小道的尽头，菲扎可以看到马舍了！他们终于安全了！他们迅速骑到院子里，跳下马，跑回房子里。

他们发现理查德·麦金太尔坐在厨房的桌子边上。他看起来很担忧。

“弗莱彻！菲扎！”他说，“你们去哪儿了？”

“没事了，理查德！”菲扎说，“我们拿到了录像，记录了斯库利做过的事！”

第108页

“是的，如果他再来找什么麻烦，我们就把录像交给警方！”弗莱彻说。

就在那时，有人从房间的一个黑暗角落走上前来。

“弗莱彻！见到你真好！你可怜的爸爸一直在为你担忧呢。嗯，既然你们在这儿，也可以给我看看那段录像，对吧？”

菲扎和弗莱彻转过身，看见罗伯特·斯库利正站在他们身后。

第 14 章　麦金太尔的大生意

第109页

斯库利用冷酷的眼神看着弗莱彻和菲扎。

“我听说你们去了帕克山那边，”他说，“所以我觉得我要来和你爸爸喝杯茶，等等你们。”

“哦，我们现在回来了，所以你可以走了。”弗莱彻说。

“不，我不能走，年轻人。没拿到你们的相机我不能走。”

“我们没有相机。”弗莱彻说。

“那就有意思了，”斯库利回答，“我的司机说你们有台相机，还说你们在拍摄我的卡车！”

弗莱彻和菲扎瞪着他。接下来理查德发话了。

“得了，孩子们，把相机给斯库利先生。”他温和地说，“我觉得你们不给的话只会把事情弄得更糟。”

菲扎拿出妈妈的手机放在桌上。

第110页

“不是相机，”她说，“是手机，真的。”

“很好，”斯库利说，“这手机很贵。”

接着，菲扎眼睁睁地看着斯库利拿起手机，把它丢到他面前桌子上的一大杯茶水里。

“现在就没有录像了。确切地说，是没有手机了！”

菲扎无法相信他的所作所为。他毁了她妈妈的手机。她妈妈会气疯的！

第111页

“那是我妈妈的！你怎么可以？”

斯库利没搭理她，站起来准备走。

“对了，我要说晚安了。为了你们不再做什么傻事，我觉得我得借点儿东西了，借此提醒你们注意点儿言行。”

“借什么？”理查德说。

“嗯，借一匹马怎么样？我想我要把那匹漂亮的黑白毛色的马带回家。”

“小金？不行！我们会报警的！”弗莱彻说。

“嗯，如果你们报了，这将是你们最后一次见到他。”

于是，理查德、菲扎和弗莱彻眼看着两个斯库利的人把小金拉到了一辆白色货车的后厢。小金使劲儿踢着他们。

“好样的，宝贝！揍他们！”弗莱彻喊道。

小金最终还是被装进车后厢里拉走了。斯库利的另一个司机在马舍大门前停放了一辆卡车，这意味着理查德的马车无法离开马舍。

“就为了防备你们再有什么蠢主意！”斯库利大笑着说。他上了车，在夜色中开走了。

第112页

他们看着斯库利没影了，三个人彻底感到无能为力。

“我要去跟着他！”弗莱彻说。

“等等！”他爸爸说，“我们不要做任何让小金陷于危险的事！”

弗莱彻气得说不出话了。菲扎突然想起了什么。

“哦！我怎么会这么傻呢！”她惊呼。

弗莱彻和理查德惊讶地看着她。

“理查德，您今晚有没有看电子邮件？”她问。

“没呢，我一直有点儿忙！”他回答。

“那好，您现在有时间看了！”

* * *

过了一会儿，理查德脸上挂着微笑回来了。

“菲扎·麦金太尔，你是个聪明的女孩儿！”他笑出了声。

“她做什么了？”弗莱彻问。

“她把用她妈妈手机录的斯库利的卡车在帕克山上的录像用电子邮件发给我了。”

这意味着他们手里还有能够用来对付斯库利的录像！

“现在我们要做什么？”弗莱彻问，还没等有人回应这个问题，外面一辆出租车停车的声音打断了他们。比利和芭布丝下了车。

第113页

“我收到你的短信了！”芭布丝说。

“发生什么事了？”比利问。

菲扎和弗莱彻简明扼要地解释了一下。

“可怜的小金！”芭布丝说。

“嗯，我觉得警方会愿意看到那段录像的备份的，是不是？”理查德说。

“您去报警吧，爸爸，而我要去斯库利家把小金弄回来！”弗莱彻说。

“我知道他住在哪里！”芭布丝说。

“好！”比利说，“走吧！”

“我们去不了！我们没法儿把马车弄出去，因为那辆卡车！”菲扎说。

“哦，别担心那个。”比利说着爬上垃圾卡车，往驾驶室里看了一下。大家都看着他。

“我提到过我爸爸是卡车司机吧？”他喊道，“他常把钥匙留在卡车里——他们也留了钥匙！”

他发动了引擎。

“可那是偷啊！”芭布丝说。

“我没有偷它！”他笑道，“我只是挪一下它。那样我们就可以把马车弄出去了。”

* * *

第114页

“这是最棒的！”弗莱彻驾着马车穿过伯明翰宁静的街道时，比利说。

“是的！”芭布丝说，“所有的出租车都应该像这样！”

菲扎暗自微笑。比利和芭布丝就像两个兴奋的小孩子坐着小马。

最终，弗莱彻驾着马车拐上了一条安静的路，路两旁是高档的大别墅。他们一栋栋的房子看过去，后来看到一栋铁门上有个大大的金色“S”的别墅。

“那就是斯库利家的房子！”芭布丝说，“我认得他的车！”

肯定是了，私家车道上停了几辆高档小汽车。比利吹了声口哨。

“很棒。”他说。

弗莱彻把马车停在了街对面，他们也躲在街对面的一棵大树后面。

“看！”他说。

斯库利的别墅门是开着的，他们可以看到一辆白色货车——正是带走小金的那辆货车。

“来吧，弗莱彻！”菲扎低声说，“咱们把你的马弄回来！”

第115页

她从马车上跳下来跑过马路，弗莱彻跟着她。他们看到两个男人从货车上爬下来，转到斯库利的房子后面不见了。门还开着，于是菲扎和弗莱彻悄悄地跑进车道，到了停货车的位置。

“小金！”弗莱彻低声说，“你在吗？”

他们听到货车里发出一声响亮的踢踏声。

“他在里面。”菲扎笑道。

弗莱彻动手去拉车厢的后门。

“没事的，宝贝，我会带你出去的。”他说。

就在这时，别墅的门徐徐关上了。他们要被锁在里面了！接着他们听到了难听的低笑声。

“你们丢东西了吗，小孩儿？”

菲扎和弗莱彻转身看见罗伯特·斯库利站在大门口。

“现在，让我想想。”他说，“第一，你们在我的地盘上。第二，你们在偷我的车。我觉得你们犯法了，是不是？要不让我们看看警察怎么想？我给他们打个电话，怎么样？”

他从上衣口袋里掏出手机。这时，他们听到又有人笑了。这次笑的是比利。他把脸贴在门上。

“我不会担心的，斯库利先生！”他喊道，“他们已经来了。”

第116页

菲扎、弗莱彻和斯库利听着。他们听到了确定无疑的警车声。车一停，车厢后门开了，理查德·麦金太尔走出来。他拿了一张光盘，上面是斯库利的卡车在帕克山地区倾倒垃圾的录像。

多么惊心动魄的夜晚啊！接下来的几天更是不同以往。罗伯特·斯库利丢掉了他的生意，因为在录像的帮助下，警方发现了在伯明翰所有绿地上倒垃圾的事都是他干的。菲扎和弗莱彻（还有比利和芭布丝）出现在各大报纸上，到处都是斗牛场酷妞和乡村牛仔的照片。

理查德·麦金太尔马车公司获得了巨大成功。人们出于各种各样的缘由来用马车，包括去上班、出去吃饭，甚至结婚！乘客数量增长了，更多的马匹和车辆添置进来帮忙。伯明翰为它那新式的“绿色”出租车服务而异常骄傲。

* * *

后来，有一个星期日，理查德·麦金太尔邀请菲扎和她的父母去他家吃午餐。他做了一顿特别的午餐。他借鉴了菲扎妈妈的菜谱。

第117页

“很好吃，理查德！”鲁贝尔说。

“嗯！”依姆兰说。

“你觉得我做的咖喱鱼怎么样，菲扎？”理查德问。

“好于……罗伯特·斯库利！”她说。

他们都笑起来，因为什么都好于罗伯特·斯库利。接着理查德忽然敛起笑容。

“听我说，孩子们。我有点儿事要告诉你们。”

他缓了一下。弗莱彻和菲扎看着他。他们都感到有点儿不对劲。

“我决定了要回萨克岛。”他说。

“可是为什么呢，爸爸？”弗莱彻说。

“伯明翰不适合我，儿子。”

“可是您不能走！”菲扎说，“生意这么成功呢！”

“哎，还有件意想不到的事！”菲扎的爸爸说，“理查德问过我们是否愿意在伯明翰经营他的业务。”

“在他回去照看萨克岛的业务的时候！”菲扎的妈妈补充说。

“那样就会有一个伯明翰麦金太尔马车公司……”依姆兰笑了起来。

第118页

“还会有一个萨克岛麦金太尔马车公司！”理查德说。

“而且如果生意顺利的话，我们甚至想买下斯库利的地！”菲扎的妈妈说。

菲扎无法相信她听到的这些。这既是个令人激动的消息，也是个令人难过的消息！

“听我说，弗莱彻，”理查德说，“你不用走，你可以和鲁贝尔、依姆兰和菲扎住在一起。”

弗莱彻愣了一下。他看了看菲扎，又看了看他爸爸。

“没事，爸爸，”他平静地说，“我跟您回家。”

他朝菲扎微笑。她也朝他笑笑，但泪水止不住从她的脸上滑落下来。

* * *

于是，菲扎再一次在理查德 · 麦金太尔整理行李箱时站在边上。这次他不是把它们放到船上，而是放到马车上；那不是她的行李，而是弗莱彻的。她帮他们把行李放进马车的时候，想起了暑假开始时她的样子——腼腆、文静，甚至可能有点儿木讷？弗莱彻 · 麦金太尔改变了她！他让她变成了现在的样子！对，比利和芭布丝是她的好朋友，但是弗莱彻远远不止是好朋友。

第119页

她太害羞了，不敢告诉他这些，但她不想让他走。

“菲扎？”

她转身看到弗莱彻站在她后面。

“嗯，我们要走了。”他说。

“好啊！”她微笑着，言不由衷。

弗莱彻看着她。他不会想念伯明翰，然而，心底里他不想离开菲扎。这个女孩儿改变了他。她让他不再那么愤懑、暴躁和粗鲁。她教会了他如何感受快乐、如何结交朋友！

但现在她看起来很开心！也许她并不在意他的离开！毕竟，他想，她还有比利！

他们面对面站着不说话。她看到一个眼睛又大又绿、鼻子上长着褐色小雀斑的男孩儿，而他看到一个眼神温暖善良、秀丽的脸庞边散着浓密的黑色卷发的女孩儿。恰在同时，他们开口了。

第120页

“我不想走，你知道。”他说。

“我不想让你走，你知道。”她说。

然后他们俩都笑了。

“但我得跟爸爸走——他没有别的亲人。”

“我理解，我也会这样做的。”

“尽量别再惹麻烦——我是说，至少我不在的时候别惹麻烦。”

“什么意思啊？”

“就是，如果在伯明翰惹什么麻烦，得我在才行。”

菲扎笑了。她突然觉得快乐多了。“如果在萨克岛惹什么麻烦，得我在才行！”她说。

“回见，斗牛场酷妞。”

“再见，乡村牛仔。”

弗莱彻·麦金太尔登上了马车，坐在他爸爸边上，不一会儿，他们就完全看不见了。